REA

D0072108

The Rhetoric of Rage

Writing About Women
Feminist Literary Studies

General Editor

Esther Labovitz
Pace University

Advisory Board

Marie Collins
Rutgers-Newark University

Doris Guilloton
New York University

Lila Hanft
Case Western Reserve University

Mark Hussey
Pace University

Helane Levine-Keating
Pace University

Vol. 22

PETER LANG
New York • Washington, D.C./Baltimore
Bern • Frankfurt am Main • Berlin • Vienna • Paris

Sondra Melzer

The Rhetoric of Rage

Women in Dorothy Parker

PETER LANG
New York • Washington, D.C./Baltimore
Bern • Frankfurt am Main • Berlin • Vienna • Paris

Library of Congress Cataloging-in-Publication Data

Melzer, Sondra.
The rhetoric of rage: women in Dorothy Parker/ Sondra Melzer.
p. cm. — (Writing about women; vol. 22)
Includes bibliographical references.
1. Parker, Dorothy, 1893–1967—Characters—Women.
2. Feminism and literature—United States—History—20th century.
3. Women and literature—United States—History—20th century. 4. Satire,
American—History and criticism. 5. Social problems in literature. 6. Anger in
literature. 7. Narration (Rhetoric). I. Title. II. Series.
PS3531.A58Z78   818'.5209—dc20   95-36389
ISBN 0-8204-3038-2
ISSN 1053-7937

Die Deutsche Bibliothek-CIP-Einheitsaufnahme

Melzer, Sondra:
The rhetoric of rage: women in Dorothy Parker/ Sondra Melzer.
- New York; Washington, D.C./Baltimore; Bern; Frankfurt am Main; Berlin;
Vienna; Paris : Lang.
(Writing about women; Vol. 22)
ISBN 0-8204-3038-2
NE: GT

The paper in this book meets the guidelines for permanence and durability
of the Committee on Production Guidelines for Book Longevity
of the Council of Library Resources.

Printed in the United States of America.

Again and again and again to Frank, who has shared my life, my love, my work for over four decades.

Always and always and always, no matter what, to my beloved family—my children, Mark and Melissa . . . always and always, no matter what.

Table of Contents

Acknowledgments

First, foremost, with all my heart and mind, to my husband Frank whom I cherish—who has believed, who has understood, who has listened, who has provided, who has strengthened, who has encouraged, who has endured, and who has always loved me. I thank you for your counsel and consent, our special life—and for this work which has come out of it.

I am grateful to every member of my doctoral committee at NYU; to Mitchell Leaska, who helped me discover this topic and whose distinguished work and provocative counsel and instruction have been, and still are, a source of inspiration and admiration to me. I was particularly fortunate in working with Joy Boyum, who cared a lot, and gave generously of her time and offered most constructive and challenging criticism that has been invaluable to me in shaping and focusing this study. I wish also to thank Lloyd Barenblatt, whose kindly interest, wisdom, and reassurance enabled me to complete my work.

It would be simple to say thank you, I am grateful to each of the rest. It would be simple; but it would not be enough. For me, this work is endowed with private meaning. It is a symbol of something that needed to be done before the life was finished. There are those who are not here to see it completed, who would have been proud.

There was a father, who knew more than he ever said in his life. There was a brave, indomitable mother who showed me that a life of sacrifice could still be filled with energy, laughter, and earthy wisdom—who first taught me how to fight back, and who made me understand that you struggle hard and love your family, no matter what. She would have been the proudest of all, and that is my deepest regret. To my second mother,

Essie, whose patient, formidable, intelligent presence still guides my better moments, despite her absence, I am, and always will be indebted.

And there is my beloved brother, Allen, a symbol too large to confine to mere words, who cared and loved and cried with me over the years of a turbulent childhood that locked us together for life in our memories so that this work and its meaning has a power to it that lives apart for both of us.

In the world of my later years, there are my children; my son Mark, who still shares my soul and my thoughts as no other, who came in my youth and grew with me; who understands more than anyone I know, the values of the human heart and spirit and who will, I am certain, carry them on in his own way, in his own time. From Melissa, whose vibrant beauty and ebullience and determination brought me laughter and pride, and who lived closely with a mother who was her teacher and who adored her, came the unfailing faith and optimism that this would be done, as indeed it is, Melissa. I thank both my children for their patience, their tolerance, their respect, their unselfish encouragement, for believing in me and for allowing me to believe in myself without ever questioning that privilege.

To my sister-in-law Barbara, who grew close to me, because she saw it was so important and brought me flowers and called me and cared, I am grateful as I am to my niece, Stephanie, who helped me when she was asked and always remembered to remember, and to Rachel who grew to understand and appreciate.

To my Harvey, who only knows how to love, and his sons, and to Arline, who was proud of everything I ever did, whether I deserved it or not, to Abe and his daughters, who support and share in the ways that only a family can, I am grateful.

To the devoted members of the English Department at Westhill High School, especially Sue, Susan, Pat, Lorrie, Harriet and Stephanie, colleagues and friends, for their unending interest, their loving concern and kindly encouragement, I am grateful, and to my students, over the years for their stimulating friendship and the joys of an academic life, I am also grateful.

I wish furthermore to express my thanks to Betty Vinci, Anne Goldstein and Dorie Johnson who typed the manuscript with patience and care, to Julie who proofread with searching detail, and to special friends whose loyalty was a constant source of encouragement, who lent their houses and their hearts when I needed them.

I wish particularly to thank Gordon Pradl for his initial counseling and assistance during my first days at NYU, my lovely friend, Joyce Schelling, for her helpful commentary, my editor Esther Labovitz for her useful, revisionary suggestions, Owen Lancer from Peter Lang for his confidence in my work, and Ann Shapiro, feminist, scholar and woman-friend for her loving support, excellent advice, and enduring interest in so much of my life.

To the many members of my family, to the unnamed friends and teachers, and to the good people through the years who have believed in me, inspired me, who have wished and waited and helped me to fulfill this promise, and who share with me its importance, I am grateful.

Chapter 1

Introduction

It is astonishing that Dorothy Parker's universe remains essentially unexplored as serious literature about women. A gifted satirist, reputed as the wittiest woman in America, Parker lived with flamboyant flair in the 1920's and become legendary as a writer of verse and short fiction that depicted uniquely female experiences.

By all accounts, she was the leading light of the small literary set centered in New York during the Jazz Age. When she published her first collection of poems, *Enough Rope*, in 1926, the book was an instant best-seller—one of the few best-selling poetry books in American history. But people bought it because the author was a media celebrity, and they seemed to appreciate it more for the voguish humor, rather than for the subtle details of the subtext, which touched upon the little, painful, and poignant struggles of women's life.

Despite Parker's popularity and reputation, or perhaps because of it, her short stories have generally been regarded as playful fictional satires, depicting stereotypical female behavior and providing little more than comic pieces of amusement for either public or academic audiences.

Although a new understanding of woman's roles in literature has begun to take hold, virtually no critics have sought to furnish serious consideration of the view of women in the works of Dorothy Parker or to explore her treatment of women from a feminist perspective.

The purpose of this work is to provide fresh perspective on the portraits of women that Dorothy Parker created and to present contemporary analyses that offer insight into female experience. This book grows out of a need to examine the fiction of Dorothy Parker as serious social commentary, to reinterpret the humor in her stories as a masking device for muted anger toward a traditional society, and to adjust the critical perspective on Parker's position as a feminist writer.

This book, furthermore, locates links between the author's life and the fiction, and aims to set the stories within a biographical context where such connections seem fruitful. Biographers agree that as a writer, Dorothy Parker drew heavily on her personal experiences as a woman. Because a woman writer has direct access to female experience, her work is imbued with a particular "consciousness" which "informs" her literature and reflects her experience and the way she perceives it. As Elaine Showalter suggests, this "consciousness" and self-awareness translates itself into literary form with specific and uniquely female patterns.

Though 'biographical speculations" can carry inherent risks, Parker's personal history, a disturbing struggle for stability and happiness, interwoven with her fictional treatment of women, furnishes a rich dimension to a feminist evaluation. Her biography was the quintessence of the Jazz Age with all its contradictions. Dazzling, flippant, reckless, and rebellious on the outside, inside, her life was marked by abject sadness, incurable pessimism, failed relationships with men, mordant moodiness, self-doubt, and self-punishment. As her life fed her fiction, her fiction elucidated elements of life.

Although, Parker's work has recently been recognized as "women's literature," and is beginning to be included in academic texts dedicated to representing women writers, nevertheless there is a notable absence of substantive scholarship on Parker in American literary criticism. Her work, critically ignored and undervalued, commands renewed attention and fresh interpretations from feminist thinkers who are seeking truthful portraits of women's lives to replace the old counterfeit models that have been handed down.

As Adrienne Rich has suggested,"redefining" women in established literature is essential as a feminist project. Feminist critics, she argues, must "re-read, re-see, re-vise," seeking valid modifications of existing images and ideals, placing them in a new context, free of old conventions. It is true that women writers may to some extent dominate their own experiences by writing about them, as Elaine Showalter and Ellen Moers argue, but still women are part of a larger cultural system which dictates not only to them, but to the way in which their work is perceived.

Hence, the arbiters of taste who praised Parker for her brisk, wry humor at her prime and then condemned her to critical disregard years later, failed in two ways to authentically assess Parker's value to contemporary feminist thinkers. The milieu from which Parker drew her subject matter may have been narrow, but her work was not trivial.

Dorothy Parker's stories seen from the perspective of modern feminist theory, shed new light on the way in which a woman's image, status, social roles, sexual behavior and relationships are to be read in literature. While drawing playful attention to the stereotypical behavior of women, Parker's ironic humor disguised implicit criticism and outrage toward a repressive and patriarchal society.

Comic stories depicting pathetic alcoholics, wisecracking "broads," submissive housewives, or love-sick girlfriends, can now be viewed from a feminist framework as socially significant statements, symptomatic of the hidden discontent and buried conflicts in women's lives.

It is important to remember that Parker operated in a male-identified group. As resident female wit and "Empress of the Algonquin Round Table," Parker matched quips and word-play with George Kaufman, Alexander Woollcott, Franklin P. Adams and Robert Benchley. She attended Long Island parties at the Fitzgeralds and later in Hollywood and abroad befriended fellow writers S. J. Perelman, Nathanial West, William Faulkner and Ernest Hemingway, whom she alternately revered and reviled.

In this atmosphere of predominantly male literati, Parker nurtured her talent for acid humor and quick repartee which she transmuted into fiction. Her short stories were marked early on by lacerating dialogue. Drawing characters from a narrow band of Eastern, American, urban, intellectual and middle to upper class society, Parker's fiction was popularized in *The New Yorker* magazine and soon identified as a type of genre, *The New Yorker* short story, characterized as smart, stylish, and amusing.

But, beneath the slick black humor, the subject matter of her work was distinctly feminist, with its preoccupation with women's problems, women's roles and women's relationships. Parker's mind bristled with female images of fashionable affectations, vacuous conversations, superficial relationships, failed romances, pointless infidelities, which she translated into sophisticated satires that had at its roots a cunning indictment of a society that permitted limited options for women and viewed them from a traditional male point of view.

It should be noted that the application of feminist theory to the works of Dorothy Parker does not assume that Parker had a specific feminist polemic or a consciously feminist intention. Indeed, what we now regard as "women's social criticism" is largely the result of Parker's unique exploration of female behavior, which inspires the contemporary critic to examine the forces in our society which drive that behavior.

An author may not set out purposely to expose aspects of sexism, or the domination of one sex by another. Although Parker does not actually present what have been called "women's issues" directly as the central focus in all of her works, nevertheless, in her portrayal of women characters, we ascertain underlying issues, situations, and attitudes of feminine concerns. In this way Parker indirectly exposes the restrictions placed upon women in a sexist society. Either consciously or without intention, Parker describes the debilitating effects of cultural oppression.

The stories in the book span Dorothy Parker's career as a short story writer, beginning in 1922 with her first published story, "Such a Pretty Little Picture," and ending with her last, "The Banquet of Crow," in 1957.

The chronological arrangement of the works enables us to observe that there is a progression and evolution in Parker's own view of women. As her life changed, her perspective changed. It would seem that as her own existence became more intolerable, Parker exhibits greater empathy with women. For example, the women of her later stories, such as Mimi McVicker ("The Lovely Leave") and Maida Allen ("The Banquet of Crow") are more mature and autonomous women than those in her earlier works. The portraits are more touching, and there are flashes in their behavior of female awareness and independence.

The stories selected are not propaganda for any particular bias towards women. Parker presents few feminine ideals;

nor does she attempt to moralize about the female condition. The stories, we must remind ourselves, are written as literature, not pedagogy. Therefore, the structural analysis of women characters, i.e., who they are, how they are presented and how they are described, reflects primarily the way the author thinks and writes about women, not necessarily the ways we would like to see women portrayed in literature. Indeed, Parker frequently reflected ambivalent, sometimes negative attitudes toward her women characters.

The informing principle behind the selection of the short stories was limited to those stories in which women were principal figures and/or women's roles were central issues in the works. While most stories selected claim women as protagonists or primary narrators, some of them were chosen because a particular artistic treatment of women was considered valuable, whether it was a positive or negative portrayal.

Many of the central conflicts in the stories revolve around the inability of women to define their relationships with men: a wife's role with a weak husband ("Such a Pretty Little Picture"), the effects of army life on a young marriage ("The Lovely Leave"), the struggle of a middle-aged woman to adapt to her husband's desertion ("The Banquet of Crow"), the results of male abuse and abandonment (Big Blonde"), the image of a lover's indifference and double standards of conduct to a young woman ("A Telephone Call"), a father's selective treatment of two daughters based on traditional patriarchal values ("The Wonderful Old Gentleman"), the tumultuous inner conflicts of a woman forced into a deceptive social situation with an unsuitable male partner ("The Waltz"), and the reactions of an unattractive woman to the hypocrisy and cruelty of traditional, and frequently also male-defined, standards of beauty ("Horsie").

Indeed, all of the stories deal with issues that at their core are concerned ultimately with the way in which men and women struggle, and in most cases fail in their relationships. However, since almost all of the stories (as almost all of Parker's stories in general) focus on a woman's response to these relationships, Parker's cynical treatment of marriage, family, and sex roles suggests that the current state of sexual arrangements lacks satisfying resolution primarily for women. For example, despite accommodations, as in "The Waltz," submissiveness as in "Mr. Durant," or adaptation as in "Big Blonde," women, for the most part, conceal their anger, outwardly play the role men expect of them, and accept whatever terms have been traditionally imposed on them.

However, we see in some cases that the actions of women such as Hazel ("Big Blonde"), Mimi McVicker ("The Lovely Leave"), and Maida Allen ("The Banquet of Crow") indicate that these women characters gradually recognize the constraints on their lives and the roles they have assumed in their relationships, and are struggling in their own way to come to terms with this awareness. They strive to achieve a consciousness of their own, one which evolves out of their experiences as women.

In addition to the pervasive question of male-female relationships, the themes of these works suggest the author's interest in a wide range of female social concerns covering a spectrum of issues from abortion ("Mr. Durant") to lesbianism ("Glory in the Daytime"), wife abuse ("Big Blonde"), and divorce ("The Banquet of Crow"). As a result of the breadth of this concern, the stories shed light on the twentieth-century image of women, as an integral part of society not only in their relationship to men, but to other women, their social place, and their cultural environment as well.

The feminist perspective, applied in this way to Parker's work, helps reveal aspects of the text which might otherwise be overlooked. Read in the light of new social awareness, Parker's treatment of women suggests more complexity and more hidden anger, particularly against men, than was previously noted by critics interested primarily in the satiric humor and urbane style of her work.

Also illuminated throughout the stories is the socialization process, which shapes not only the sex roles that individuals assume are a fixed and natural part of our society, but the forces both direct and indirect that structure the male and female temperaments in accordance with these roles. As Kate Millet suggests, the status accorded to men and women derives from the various values assigned to maintaining civilization.[1]

The female characters portrayed in many of the stories, though responsible for their own actions, are generally depicted

within a social framework rooted in specifically socially defined roles, the result of what Karen Horney calls, the "culture
complex."[2] Parker's characterizations of women may appear
cynical, amusing, harsh,or stereotypical, but beneath the humor, the author affords the reader the opportunity to explore
the origins of these roles, and the condition of women's lives
which have often led to their behavior, whether aggressive,
self-centered, pathetic, or submissive.

The stories bear out the view held by feminist writers suggested earlier, that this stereotypic behavior, seemingly in
women's nature, is often a woman character's strategy for cop-
ing with a set of circumstances or an environment that presents limited alternatives associated with her condition.

Dominance (Mrs. Wheelock), submissiveness (Mrs.
Durant), hysteria (narrator in "A Telephone Call"), bitchiness
(Hattie), self-centeredness (Camilla), as portrayed in these stories, are traceable in part to the repressive and limiting environment of their lives as women, which cause them to act in
ways that are traditionally, but perhaps mistakenly, regarded
as endemic to their female nature.

Furthermore, while the two narrators in "The Waltz" and
"A Telephone Call" are clearly outraged and abused as a result
of their disappointment and humiliating experiences with men,
we must bear in mind that these women exhibit another form
of social conditioning that Horney calls "the soil for the growth
of masochistic phenomena," a certain "preparedness in women
for a masochistic conception of their role."[3] Both these women
appear to have a history of unhappy affairs with men and yet
cling to arrangements which provoke their degradation and
mistreatment.

Beneath the worldly bravado as a public celebrity, Parker
herself dealt with the pain of being a woman. Broken love affairs that led to a string of suicide attempts, failed marriages,
traumatic abortions, depression and drinking testified to the
terrible despair of her private hell, a female place of insecurity,
loneliness and fragility.

Feminist critics argue that cultural factors are so powerful an influence, that it is hard to imagine that any woman can
avoid some degree of masochistic behavior in her relationship
with men. Parker's characterizations of these emotionally de-

pendent women are among her most unforgettable portraits, no longer regarded as comic "clinging vines," but viewed as an effect of male ideologies that promote submissive traits more frequently desired by men.

Certainly it must be acknowledged that there are other causes that contribute to the restrictive behavior of women. Without minimizing the influences that social and cultural factors exert on women, or the effects of internalized patriarchal ideals, there are inherent "anatomical-physiological-psychological" characteristics innate to women and feminine development that govern their lives as well. Phyllis Rose, for example, acknowledges the "shadowy internal prohibitions and emotional phantoms"[4] that haunted Virginia Woolf. The precise weight of these two groups of factors cannot be assessed, nor was it the intention of this study to do so. It is clear, however, that there is a confluence of forces at work in the lives of women that must be addressed by contemporary thinkers. Parker provides material to build a case for a feminist examination of those synergetic forces that forge a woman's history.

As previously pointed out, Parker's characters are not necessarily sympathetic. Indeed, like the domineering Mrs. Wheelock ("Such a Pretty Little Picture"), the vacuous Camilla ("Horsie"), and the bitchy Hattie ("The Wonderful Old Gentlemen"), they are often negative and unappealing. Nevertheless, Parker's perceptions of women help raise contemporary consciousness as to the causes of why women are this way. Thus, negative images and stereotypical images alike can be subject to analysis derived from new techniques of feminist criticism recently formulated and relatively uncharted during the author's lifetime. Since Parker's basic genre was satire, we must realize she presents a particular and unusual form of feminist awareness, not necessarily in her exhortations, but in her perceptions.

Obviously, prior critics have acknowledged the presence and portrayal of women characters in Parker's work. Still, as this study illustrates, the application of feminist theory calls for new approaches towards the way that women characters define themselves and their lives in fiction, and fresh understanding of the literary strategies of women writers who have generated a female tradition and style of their own.

Parker's fiction in particular provides a paradigm for the study of "women's language." Each of the works in this study deals not only with women, but also contains the language traits, lexicon, speech patterns, vocabulary, idioms, and forms that have been associated with women's language. The topic of language and the sexes has drawn a wave of critical attention recently, both in published works and in ongoing research.

Robin Lakoff's book, *Language and Woman's Place*, suggests that the overall effect of "women's language"—meaning "both language restricted in use to women and language descriptive of women alone"—is that it submerges a woman's identity by "denying her the means of expressing herself strongly and encouraging her in expressions of 'triviality.'" This linguistic phenomenon has the ultimate effect of systematically denying women access to power and encouraging them to feelings of inadequacy.

Parker's parodic and satiric language, the lexical traits of her female characters, viewed from the rigors of a feminist tradition, reflect these patterns of women's speech, now understood as the result of cultural conditioning, but nevertheless provocative of contemptuous stereotyping about women and their womanish ways.

Parker's career as a writer had a brilliant beginning, but sadly, an early demise. Despite the fact that Parker lived a protracted life, her powers as a writer diminished and her bitterness increased. By 1967 the majority of her friends were gone or alienated, and her popularity had become part of a vogue that had vanished. Unable to write, aging, ostensibly impoverished, assuaged by alcohol, and comforted by the only companion whom she had not estranged, her poodle, Troy, Parker died alone and in obscurity in a hotel room in New York, having long outlived her fame. In an irony that would have pleased her, most people who read of her passing thought that she had been dead for some time.

The literary audience of her own time recognized and celebrated her lively and vivacious wit. Her portraits of women were viewed as paradigms of satiric genius. It remains, however, for contemporary feminist thinkers to probe beneath the brilliant humor to discover the subtle rage and elusive wisdom, that consciously or inadvertently etched with canny skill the discontent of women's lives and the prescriptive environment in which they lived. The reader is invited to join in this discovery.

Parker's work suggests at its deepest level, that it is a very serious thing to be a funny woman.

Notes

1 Millet argues that, "however muted its present appearance may be, sexual dominion obtains nevertheless as perhaps the most pervasive ideology of our culture and provides its most fundamental concept of power." *Sexual Politics* (New York: Ballantine Books, 1969), p. 33.

2 Karen Horney, *Feminine Psychology* (New York: W. W. Norton & Co., 1967), p. 230.

3 Horney, p. 231.

4 Phyllis Rose, *Women of Letters, A Life of Virginia Woolf* (New York: Oxford University Press, 1978) p. xiv.

Chapter 2

Selected Short Stories of
Dorothy Parker

Portrait of a Marriage:
"Such a Pretty Little Picture"

"Such a Pretty Little Picture"[1] was Dorothy Parker's first short story. A slice-of-life vignette that appeared in *The Smart Set* magazine in 1922, the work portrays the dead and passionless marriage of a suburban couple, but more importantly prefigures an abiding interest in the anguished relationship between the sexes that was to command Dorothy Parker's attention as a writer most of her life.

Etched in this story are many of the provocative images of the failure of honest and satisfying domestic relationships which were to appear repeatedly in Parker's later works. The wife was portrayed as domineering and emasculating; the husband was undistinguished and oppressed; the marriage was a travesty.

The caustic parody of ideal American married life was written by a twenty-nine year old Parker, who was already in her ascendancy as a principle of the Algonquin Club Round Table, or the "Vicious Circle," as it became known by New York's glittering literary society. An assertive woman with a sharp "masculine" humor, she was writing and performing for a predominantly male audience at the Round Table. She was at this time also intermittently separated from Edwin Parker II, a shy, handsome, quiet, young man, who had returned from the war in Europe in 1919 and was no match for his wife or his wife's witty new companions. It does not appear accidental that as Parker's marriage to Eddie disintegrated, she turned at this time to the subject of domestic anguish in her writing. Beneath the brittle humor, the portrait of the fictional marriage laid bare striking analogies to Parker's own marital problems.

In its simple outline, the story is about Mr. Wheelock, a thirty-seven year old husband and father, who fantasizes escape from his vapid existence while clipping his suburban hedge, as his wife and child watch from the spotless porch of their neat stucco house. Caught in the gracious evening light that belies the undercurrents of pain, the portrait presents a false paradigm of domestic bliss to two passing neighbors. Frustrated and imprisoned in his life, as his surname suggests, Mr. Wheelock is bored by his meaningless job in the city, bored by his domineering wife and bored by his dull clod of a daughter.

In spite of the materialistic pleasures of his modern existence, he experiences incongruously a sense of anomie. He has no one who understands him, few friends that he can talk to, and his shallow suburban life affords him only business and social acquaintances. His relationships lack importance, so he dreams as he clips his hedge that one day he'll be able to say "Oh hell" (p. 162) and walk away from this superficial life and make a new start.

Lost in recurring reverie and the routine of his clipping, Mr. Wheelock submerges present reality and moves deeper into the private fantasy of departure that has taken hold of him:

> It was about a man who lived in a suburbs. Every morning he had gone to the city on the 8:12, sitting in the same seat in the same car, and every evening he had gone home to his wife on the 5:17, sitting in the car. He had done this for twenty years of his life. And then one night he didn't come home. He never went back to his office any more. He just never turned up again. (p. 162)

The passing neighbors, Mr. and Mrs. Coles, who see Mr. Wheelock reverently at work, observed by his wife and daughter, pause on their evening constitutional to characterize the tableau as "such a pretty little picture" (p. 166), the quintessence, they are satisfied, of American suburban success.

Ironically, the wife, the child, and the neighbors, who see only the surface appearance of the marriage, think of it as conventional and hence ideal, a metaphor of Parker's personal dread.

"Such a Pretty Little Picture" affords the reader the opportunity to examine women from a variety of vantage points. The story unwinds through a series of narrations: through a distant objective narration, through the wife's blind conversation, and through the inner thoughts of the husband. Told predominantly from the husband's point of view, as narrator-observer, the story ostensibly revolves around Mr. Wheelock's entrapment at the hands of a nagging wife. But the reader cannot ignore certain questions of causality, which transform the facts of the story into the meaning of the plot. What has caused the marriage to fail? Why does the husband subject himself to dominance? The principle of causality forces us beyond the husband's manifest despair and leads us to the deeper more elusive issue of the wife's satiric role as the stereotypical bovine, emasculating *Hausfrau.*

In this first work, which has received very little critical attention, we are provided with a glimpse of the ways in which Parker's acerbic portrayal of American stereotypes reflects scorn not only toward established "values," but on a deeper level, toward a traditional patriarchal society that prescribed these "values."

What strikes the reader in this initial piece is that this bitter portrait of a marriage appears to manifest the author's negative, even contemptuous attitude toward women. Physically repulsive, intellectually vapid, manipulative, predictable and boring, the females in the story invite little compassion.

The question arises at once: Why is Mrs. Wheelock, Dorothy Parker's first full-scale fictional woman character, such an objectionable female? Are we simply to assume that this unappealing image is a reflection of Parker's own negative view of women in general?

Perhaps not. To perceive Mrs. Wheelock as merely an anti-feminist character, the extension of Parker's own cynical view of women, would be both limited and insufficient in light of contemporary feminist perspective. Mrs. Wheelock is clearly an unsympathetic character, negatively portrayed from the outset. She is also, admittedly, responsible for the choices she makes as a wife, a mother, and a woman. It would be pointless to argue that she is a helpless victim of circumstances, when she is so evidently the architect of her own aggressive personality. Yet, there are forces at work within her marriage, as well as outside of her domestic relationships, that encourage Mrs. Wheelock's domineering and male-destructive behavior, and thereby perpetuate the absurd stereotype that Parker presents.

The negative image that Parker depicts may be related to factors both inherent in Mrs. Wheelock's female nature and existing in the social organization in which she has developed. The overlapping of these factors, for it would seem that no one factor is ever solely responsible for behavioral development, contributes to a concatenation of causative factors. In light of new social awareness regarding the literary lives of women, such a confluence of factors should not be ignored.

If we track the progression of each character's thoughts and words, as they interact with each other, the meaning of the story emerges not simply as a study of male boredom and female shrewishness, but on a more subtle level, as the first of Parker's satiric treatments of women whose behavior may be largely a response to society's narrow vision of acceptable "proper" female roles. Explicitly, it is the story of a man's existence with an absurdly domineering wife; implicitly, it is the saga of mutual entrapment in what appears to be a sadomasochistic relationship of classic dominance and subservience. Clearly, Parker's conception of women emerging in her first narrative rendering, was intertwined in some way at this time with her sense of herself and her experiences, as she projected into fiction the destructive potential of an overbearing woman committed to a stifling domestic existence with an introverted man.

In 1922, the young Dorothy Parker may not have been prepared to reveal herself directly in fiction, but the links to her life are evident. It was generally known that Parker always wrote about her own experiences or drew upon portraits of friends, who later, and with justification, frequently joined the burgeoning ranks of her enemies. Indeed, she seldom created fictional characters that were not based on people she knew, and subsequently abused.

Her celebrity status at *Vanity Fair* was growing as a result of her cleverly written captions, reviews and articles. The public loved her witticisms. But it was at the Algonquin Club luncheons that Parker nurtured and perfected her verbal quick hitting comic scenarios of barbs, punch lines, and smart retorts, delivered with vaudevillian timing.

She had become adept at wicked put-downs and had developed a repertoire of obscenities and dead-pan insults. She excelled at wisecracks and puns, earning herself a reputation as a treacherously funny woman. She flattered people to their faces and criticized them behind their back.

Her precarious marriage to the reserved Edwin Pond Parker II, a descendant from a proper family of Connecticut ministers, and a ninth generation Protestant whose name had provided Dorothy Rothschild a cherished instant conversion from her hated half-Jewish background, was put in growing jeopardy.

Eddie had become addicted to morphine in the Army as an ambulance driver in the war, and returned to his wife unsettled, repressed, and painfully withdrawn. Stories circulated that there were suicide attempts and Dorothy had found him on several occasions passed out cold with his head in the gas oven. After treatments and sanitoriums, he succeeded in overcoming his morphine addiction only to develop a serious drinking problem.

When Eddie asked Dorothy to return to Hartford with him with the hope of resolving his growing problem with alcohol and re-entering the insurance business, Dorothy refused to go with him, preferring the vitality and excitement of the New York literary scene. Donald Ogden Stewart, fellow member of the Round Table, commented to John Keats, Parker's biographer, "What in God's name would she do in Hartford? Can you see her going to Hartford with Eddie Parker after she had begun to meet people like Benchley and Sherwood and FPA and Woollcott?"[2]

Eddie was increasingly uncomfortable, embarrassed, conspicuously inadequate and out of place in Parker's vitriolic circle. Parker began to concoct stories about him, and regaled her friends with "stupid Eddie" mishaps. "I want you to meet my little husband,"[3] Parker quipped to her companions, resonating the pathetic figure of the emasculated Mr. Wheelock, who was no doubt already forming in Parker's mind.

James Gaines theorizes that Robert Benchley, Parker's closest friend throughout the Algonquin years, also bore an uncanny resemblance to Mr. Wheelock, in "Such a Pretty Little Picture," in his role as "householder" and in his inability to break finally from family obligations.[4] Ironically, it was Benchley's friendship that appears to have driven Edwin Parker away permanently.

The meticulous domesticity that Parker dreaded and derided all her life (she was never to keep an orderly house and hated to cook), was incarnated in the obsessive character, Adelaide Wheelock. We first meet Adelaide on the steps of the spotless porch.

> She was not a tall woman, and since the birth of her child she had gone over from a delicate plumpness to a settled stockiness. Her brown hair, though abundant, grew in an uncertain line about her forehead. It was her habit to put it up in curlers at night, but the crumps never came out in the right place. It was arranged with perfect neatness, yet it suggested that it had been done up and got over with as quickly as possible . . . She was wanting to tell people, somewhat redundantly, that she never employed any sort of cosmetics. She had unlimited contempt for women who sought to reduce their weight by dieting, cutting from their menus such nourishing items as creams and puddings and cereals. (p. 139)

Passionately immaculate, obsessed with "Perfect neatness" (p. 154), redolent of germicidal soap, she deplored cosmetics and righteously prided herself on a "no nonsense" air, which she unequivocally regarded as a virtue, as did her many admiring friends. Her preoccupation with cleanliness and order tells us a good deal about her personal chemistry. It is a clue to an aggressive and domineering nature held in control and sublimated into an acceptable womanly social preoccupation with domesticity, that may, according to Simone de Beauvoir, border on perversion.[5]

> She was going over all the buttons before he wore the garments, sewing them on more firmly . . . She worked with quick, decided movements, compressing her lips each time the thread made a slight resistance to her deft jerks. (p. 159)

The fact that Mrs. Wheelock sews the buttons on before they come off is a detail that cannot be ignored. She works with an open aggressiveness on her chores, finding ways to inflict her will, even upon inanimate objects. Mr. Wheelock, on the other hand, is reported to be "notoriously poor at doing anything around the house" (p. 158).

Conversely, the men of Mrs. Wheelock's acquaintance were adept at putting up shelves, repairing locks, making storage boxes, while Mr. Wheelock, admittedly, was inefficient in such matters. When they were first married, he had allowed himself to become the butt of jokes about his helplessness, even posing as more inefficient than he was to make the jokes better. But, "Mr. Wheelock had begun to feel that there was something rather effeminate about his lack of interest in such things." (p. 158)

Mr. Wheelock's growing sense of inadequacy juxtaposed with Mrs. Wheelock's abundant sense of efficiency suggests a reversal of traditionally identified sexual roles. Hence, in various ways, Adelaide punishes her husband for his "effeminateness," and his refusal to assert himself.[6]

> Her most popular anecdote was of how, the past winter, he had gone out and hired a man to take care of the furnace, after seven years losing struggle with it. She had an admirable memory and as often as she related the story, she never dropped a word of it. Even now, in the late summer, she could hardly tell it for laughing. (p. 158)

Sensing her husband's weakness and finding no resistance, she forges ahead deceptively and relentlessly against her mate, cultivating his dependence on her and thereby her power over him with a mixture of satisfaction and resentment. She refers to him as "Daddy," and alerts the neighbors that she and her daughter watch over him at his hedge-cutting, for fear "He might cut his little self with the shears" (p. 165). She talks to him in patronizing female euphemisms, emasculating him with slavish motherly gestures, running his house, looking after his clothing, cooking his meals without complaint or losing her temper, or inspiring in him the slightest manly emotions. She was in all a "sterling woman, an utterly faithful wife" (p. 164), the most subtle of enemies.[7]

We derive further insight into Mrs. Wheelock's nature, if we examine closely the phrase that apparently expresses Mrs. Wheelock's fear that Mr. Wheelock "might cut his little self with the shears" (p. 165). What connotative suggestions regarding Mrs. Wheelock's real wishes for her husband are buried in that silly, childish gibe? In view of her emasculating nature, is this a latent hope, offered in jest, that Mr. Wheelock *would* (emphasis added) indeed "cut his little self with the shears," and thereby fulfill literally the utmost expression of her intrinsically castrating disposition? A writer of Parker's celebrated glibness certainly was capable of such innuendo.

Conversely, Mr. Wheelock, bound and locked emotionally and sexually, thinks of his wife significantly as "sterling," linking her with phonetic inferences of sterile and/or sterilizing. He furthermore characterizes her as not faithful, but "*utterly faithful*" (emphasis added), an overloaded expression in view of the fact that one is either faithful or not faithful. The linguistic intensity hints at Mrs. Wheelock's darker motives as vaguely perceived by her husband, motives that strangulate his manhood and deny him power and potency as a master of his own home.

Interestingly, Mrs. Wheelock's tyranny over the household may actually serve to underscore the smallness of her life and the restriction of her power, which is confined within the bounds of her own home.

There is in Adelaide a militant energy that simultaneously terrifies and confuses Mr. Wheelock. After all, "She never lost her temper, she was never depressed, never ill" (p. 164). He did not have the shadow of an excuse for leaving her. "People," he thought, "would invent an excuse for him. They would say there must be another woman" (p. 164).

As though the actual thought of another woman triggers an involuntary physical response, Mr. Wheelock at that instant "frowned and snipped at an obstinate young twig" (p. 164) in a revealing gesture of unaccustomed aggressiveness. "Good Lord, the last thing he wanted was another woman" (p. 164), a penetrating echo perhaps, to his lost sense of manhood and his own expressed fears of "effeminateness."

"What he wanted was that moment when he realized he could do it, when he could lay down the shears . . ." (p. 164). Precisely what is meant by the phrase, "lay down the shears"? If we argue that the act of cutting the hedge with the shears constitutes the only masculine role Mr. Wheelock is permitted, as cited earlier, then the choice to "lay down the shears," i.e., to relinquish his male image, suggests an abiding desire to surrender his masculinity. In the end, the effect of Adelaide's dominance seems unequivocal. What the narrator seeks is an acquittal, and escape from women, altogether.

This notion is reinforced by exploring Wheelock's attitude toward his five-year old daughter. Significantly called Sister by Mrs. Wheelock since the child's birth, she is an ugly, sickly, dull, and obedient child who never inspired the fierce thrill of fatherly love from Mr. Wheelock. Petted and overindulged by her mother, Sister is denied identity and personality as an individual. Instead, she is monotonously satisfied to be her mother's nameless appendage, dutiful, unquestioning, sensible, well-mannered, and exquisitely cautious of her bodily well-being. The child made Wheelock feel "ill at ease" (p. 160) and vaguely irritated. He had acknowledged to himself from the first that he "did not like Sister as a person" (p. 160).

In these lines we recognize the potency of Mrs. Wheelock in the family constellation. Parker's first fictional portrait of women implied power—power, however, dressed in matriarchal trappings. The parody of the overbearing woman that Parker presents exposes the most intimidating and manipulative aspects of Mr. Wheelock's personality. Nevertheless, the suffocating maternalism that Mrs. Wheelock assumes in her role toward her husband, ensnares her as well,and simultaneously functions to restrict her as a woman in the most conventional ways. In effect, Mrs. Wheelock has chosen her own form of containment. Her sphere of influence is narrow. Her concerns are trivial, her conversation petty.

Mrs. Wheelock speech throughout is rife with "women's language,"[8] trivialities, repetitions, euphemisms, empty adjectives, and references to women's "subjects." Consider the following excerpts:

> "Doctor Mann says we are going ahead finely. I saw his automobile passing the house this morning—he was going to see Mr. Warren, his rheumatism's coming along nicely—and I called him a minute to look us over." (p. 165)

> "He said there's no need for those t-o-n-s-i-l-s to c-o-m-e-o-u-t, Mrs. Wheelock called. But I thought, soon's it gets a little cooler, some time next month, we'd just run in to the city and let Doctor Sturges have a look at us. I was telling Daddy, 'I'd rather be on the safe side,' I said." (pp. 165-166)

Parker's exaggerated portrait, stereotypical female lexicon and mockery of the language of women is a vicious portrayal that functions not only as humor, but more importantly as a perception of female behavior, viewed in the social expectations of a traditionally defined society.

In her first published story, ironically entitled to signal indictment of American values, Parker uses a ridiculous woman character to criticize the choices of a dominant female personality tempted to acquire strength through the diminution of her husband's confidence and power. The cognizant reader might be encouraged to join Parker not in denouncing women per se, but rather in recognizing the ludicrous and often corruptive effects of women who have lived out their marital roles as their husband's housekeepers and caretakers.[9] Mrs. Wheelock actively lacks meaningful identity of her own and though apparently a powerful force in the house, "She is rarely viewed in her true powerlessness far removed from any source of significant decision making."[10]

On the one hand, the parody of social pattern, e.g., fur sales, talk of doctors, repetitious inessentials, and the maternal portrait of Mr. Wheelock as " Daddy" seems harmless and ritualistic; on the other hand, the language masks contempt for Mr. Wheelock's weakness and reiterates Mrs. Wheelock's dominion over the household, which has become entirely womanized. Parker understood dominance over men. She incarnated it and simultaneously relished it and regretted it in herself. She was to say later in life, "I was just a little Jewish girl trying to be cute."[11]

On the basis of gender-determined behavior, stereotypical language conventions deny both parties direct communication and access to truth. Mr. Wheelock, dutiful husband, submerges his thoughts and resentments in unspoken reveries of escape and perfunctory responses; while Mrs. Wheelock, maternal wife, subverts her aggression and desire for dominance in female deceptions of public politeness and stereotypical accommodations. Disclosure and forthright honesty is impossible. There exists on the basis of language a central tension between husband and wife.

While Parker's portrayal of Mrs. Wheelock is a caricature of a domineering *Hausfrau*, it may also be viewed as the portrait of an authoritative woman, whose aggressive behavior in her marriage is a response to a weak and unsatisfying partner.[12] Parker's satiric purpose and technique permitted her to ridicule the woman, drawing sympathy for the dominated husband, yet beneath the satire is the image of a militant female whose sublimated energy expressed itself in intense domesticity and emasculation. Nevertheless, Mrs. Wheelock remains essentially unsympathetic, the functional architect of a marriage that is neither healthy nor appealing.

It is true that Mrs. Wheelock found vicarious satisfaction for her need to control, ruling with absolute dominion within the narrow sphere of the home. But, intense domesticity is a female trap and Mrs. Wheelock is both a perpetrator and a victim. By contrast, Parker's own hatred of domesticity expressed itself in slovenly acts of personal rebellion. She was known to eat bacon raw, rather than cook it. Her drawers and closets were a mess, her home untidy, and her dogs left unhousebroken. Mrs. Wheelock parodied in fiction the opposite extreme of Parker's version of herself as homemaker. Both the fiction and the fact dramatize Parker's disdain for mythologized womanhood.

Parker's feminist concerns in this instance, reflect an interest in the condition of women's lives and the nature of their roles, with no obligation to present exclusively sympathetic portrayals of women or feminist ideals. Parker shows Mrs. Wheelock as she perceives her, a manipulative and stereotypical shrew, fulfilling her role in a silly domestic life.

Indeed, the marriage is a travesty. The negative and destructive characterization of Mrs. Wheelock appears even worse than the weak and pathetic characterization of Mr. Wheelock. However, Parker's apparent contempt for Mrs. Wheelock is not necessarily a mandate against all women. Seen from the feminist perspective of social criticism, "destructive" female behavior can often be seen as a response to certain conditions in spheres of life where the estimation of women, on the whole, is inferior to men and where economic and social dependency through marriage are embedded in cultural patterns.

As a satirist, Parker created caricature, exaggerated Mrs. Wheelock's objectionable qualities, without developing insight into her personality or the complexity of the world around her.

This is not to say that the unflattering portrait does not reflect a confluence of forces to which Mrs. Wheelock responds and contributes as a married woman.

It appears that Parker is chiefly concerned in this story, not merely with the portrayal of a wife's role, but with the difficulty of the relationship between the sexes, and the effects of a constricted domestic life on both men and women. The ironic authorial vision of a man and woman locked in the bonds of a ludicrous matrimonial travesty in "Such a Pretty Little Picture" dramatizes the disparity between the ideal and the reality of the revered institution of marriage. Parker no doubt sensed, in the recurring image of the confining "hedge," literally rising between the couple, stubbornly resisting the shears, an aesthetic symbol of the emotional barriers, the psychic walls between the sexes.

Mr. Wheelock, whose first name remains significantly unknown, Adelaide Wheelock, and Sister Wheelock, remain fixed in the seductive matriarchy of their lives. The title, "Such a Pretty Little Picture," which draws descriptively on what are generally regarded as "female" adjectives, instructs the reader in Parker's closing irony. In creating a specifically negative perception of Mrs. Wheelock, Parker projects in this piece an early cynicism toward marriage and parenthood. In the end, it is the imposing image of Mrs. Wheelock, ensconced on her suburban porch, attended by her dutiful daughter, magisterially surveying the unclipped hedge and the bent figure of her husband, that haunts the imagination and gives symbolic weight to the reader's first full-scale view of Parker's women.

This deadly portrait of matrimony certainly is identifiable as a projection of the personal events unfolding in Parker's life. Parker's cynical portrayal of wedlock and parenthood was written precisely at the time that Parker's own marriage was unraveling. By the spring of 1922 Eddie left for Hartford without Dorothy. No longer able to endure Parker's open disregard and belittling, Eddie sought to start his life anew. Dorothy, dismayed despite the fact that the break had been anticipated, worked feverishly through the summer on "Such A Pretty Little Picture," rewriting and revising it laboriously in longhand, as she was to do with her fiction throughout her life.

Dorothy's career as a short story writer had begun.[13] The narrative, which she later referred to as the "best thing she ever wrote"[14] transmitted into fiction some of the disturbing elements of her own failed domestic life.

Eddie returned to New York once more in January for a brief, futile attempt at reconciliation. Ultimately, Eddie remarried and settled in Hartford as a businessman. The divorce was not finalized until 1928, and thereafter Eddie never spoke of his marriage to Parker for the remainder of his life. As for Dorothy, she seldom mentioned Eddie after his departure but was known later to comment characteristically, "I married to change my name from Rothschild to Parker—that is all there was to it."[15]

Male Myths and Misogny: "Mr. Durant" (1924)

The period between late 1922 and 1923 was to be one of the most tumultuous interludes in Parker's life. While her reputation for brusque and robust rhetoric flourished, Parker's personal life disintegrated. With Eddie gone, Parker sought a variety of fleeting affairs with men. All proved brief, boring and unsatisfactory. However, Charles MacArthur, son of a church minister from Pennsylvania, exclusively educated and somewhat aloof, penetrated the notoriously tough veneer and attracted Parker in an immediate and intense love affair. A twenty-seven-year-old newspaperman and aspiring playwright, Charles Gordon MacArthur was handsome and irresistibly charming, with a reckless sense of humor and a reputation as a hearty drinker, a playboy and a womanizer.

Alexander Woollcott, self-appointed mentor of promising literary talent, who regarded MacArthur as a fabulous discovery, took an interest in guiding his career, and introduced Charles to the crowd at the Algonquin. It seems clear that Woollcott meant to play matchmaker and bring Parker and MacArthur together, even though he was well aware that MacArthur was married. Though geographically separated and seemingly estranged from his wife, Carol, MacArthur wrote affectionate letters to her regularly and did not appear to pursue divorce. By all accounts, Parker fell hopelessly in love with MacArthur in a relationship that according to her friend Anita Loos, "was as fervid as it was ill-advised."[16] The affair ended in disaster.

Parker had been warned by her friends that Charlie was after all "Charlie," a flirtatious roué, who, as Loos reported, "liked all women, and no special woman."[17] Benchley told Parker to forget him, and Ben Hecht, who later collaborated with MacArthur, allowed that he was a dashing and intriguing fellow with a poet's spirit, but there ". . . was also a wildness in Charlie, . . . well-policed . . . He had to feed the daemon in him a great deal of liquor to keep it in line . . ."[18]

Warnings to the contrary, Parker persisted with MacArthur, believing that they would marry after Dorothy's divorce was finalized and MacArthur untangled his own marital affairs. The woman that Woollcott had described as a "blend of Little Nell and Lady Macbeth,"[19] was soon writing sentimental love poetry to Charlie, and acting like a romantically smitten schoolgirl. The couple were seen everywhere together, and to the amazement of the Round Tablers, Parker, whose savage put-downs were feared as much as admired, behaved in the manner of one of her own caricatures, innocently clinging to a man who casually moved from one conquest to another.

It appears that everyone in Parker's circle knew that MacArthur was seeing other women, while Parker chose, outwardly at least, to ignore his infidelities to her. In an act that would prove to be a cynical prophecy of unfolding events, Parker at this time wrote "Unfortunate Coincidence," a poetic transcription of her growing inner apprehensions:

> By the time you swear you're his,
> Shivering and sighing,
> And he vows his passion is
> Infinite, undying—
> Lady, make a note of this:
> One of you is lying.[20]

Before the year was over, Parker came to the tormenting realization that she was pregnant, and that, at the same time, Charles MacArthur was clearly losing interest in her. Her smoking and drinking increased as her despair deepened. Her friends became worried about her, and according to Benchley she wept endlessly. She appeared paralyzed by the situation, reluctant to abort the fetus on the one hand, and desperately hoping that MacArthur would return on the other. Biographer Marion

Meade, reports "She found herself, at the age of twenty-nine, married, pregnant, and carrying the child of another man, also married."[21]

Prolonging an abortion as long as possible, Parker entered a New York hospital with alleged stomach trouble where the doctors performed a legal, medically controlled abortion, arranged for a very high fee. The event left Parker with deep psychological scars. She came to believe that because of her delay in seeking an abortion, the embryo had already formed hands which she was convinced she saw in the fetal material. Her guilt festered, her depression grew, nourished by grief and alcohol, and despite the staunch friendships and witty, albeit vacuous verbiage of her fellow Algonquinites, Parker's mind turned to thoughts of suicide. It did not help that cruel gossip circulated that MacArthur had contributed thirty dollars toward the cost of the abortion. Parker would later quip sarcastically that it was like "Judas making a refund."[22] Reckless remarks notwithstanding, Parker's first emotional breakdown was already in its formative stage.

"It's not the tragedies that kill us," Parker said, "It's the messes. I can't stand messes."[23] By the age of thirty, neither married nor divorced, drinking heavily and prone to contemplation of suicide, Parker's bad experiences were rooted in depression, contempt for men, self-hatred and self-pity. Her life had become what she reviled—a "mess"—and her unrelieved anger found its way to print in 1924 in the bitter portrait of "Mr. Durant," a harrowing expression of female rage.

Drawn directly from the recent painful events in Parker's life, "Mr. Durant"[24] deals with the subject of adultery and abortion. Told in a third-person narrative, it chronicles Mr. Durant's male chauvinism and cruelty toward women.

When Mr. Durant, a minor administrator in a rubber works, learns that Rose, his secretary, with whom he has been having a passing affair, is pregnant, he resentfully agrees to partially pay for the abortion to fix things up. Although he prides himself on his worldliness in these matters, Mr. Durant ultimately depends on Ruby, Rose's friend, to make the final arrangements. Filled with satisfaction at the outcome, he indifferently sends Rose off, chuckling to himself, "Well, that's that" (p. 41).

A few days later, in a gesture that reverberates his treatment of Rose, Mr. Durant refuses to allow his children to keep a newly found stray female dog. He vows to throw the dog out at night, making it clear to his obedient wife that he "wouldn't give a she-dog house room for any amount of money" (p. 146). It would be disgusting, he insists, to have a female around that might "become pregnant and have puppies" (p. 46). As he strolls to dinner that night with his arm around his wife, he smiles complacently with the knowledge that everything was all fixed up and ready for a "fresh start" (p. 46).

"Mr. Durant" provides a monodimensional view of women from the filtered consciousness of a singularly insensitive, chauvinistic man. The reader is allowed entry to the thoughts and actions of Mr. Durant, the titular head of the story, as he deals with a traditional "woman's issue," abortion. As a result, his stereotypical behavior as a man enables the reader to perceive women from a male point of view in a way that would not be possible if the story were told in a woman's voice, or in fact, dominated by the personality of women characters. The main literal character is male, but the subject of concern is the male's view of women, treated ironically.

The dominant presence of Mr. Durant in the story further functions as a means to examine the source of Mr. Durant's attitude toward his lover, his wife, his female fantasies, and his speculations on strange women and little girls. Hence, the story offers the reader a male view of women that reflects Mr. Durant's private thoughts in conjunction with his public behavior.

Much of the effect of the story depends on language. The linguistic rendering of the inner life of Mr. Durant from the outset intimates the hypocrisy and insincerity of his nature and keys us in to his attitude toward women. Caught up in the cliched posturing he believes is correct, proper, and moral, he deceives himself, unwittingly perhaps, in a language that denies authentic experience. Often the objects of satire, people who use such masking language[25] may not be aware, or are only vaguely aware, that they are not only concealing authentic reality but creating a different reality, one that does not coincide with the words they utter, the thoughts they think, or the gestures they make.

Mr. Durant is presented to us in the opening line of the story ten days after Rose's departure, awaiting a street car after work. He is in an ecstatic state of newly achieved peace of mind. In the second sentence, the reader is informed that Mr. Durant is experiencing a palpable feeling of contentment, which the author describes as "warm and soft," as though he were wrapped in a luxurious "new and expensive cloak" (p. 35). Why has Parker chosen metaphorically to surround Mr. Durant in a "cloak" so early in the story? Why is the visual effect of the word "cloak," in juxtaposition to the first word of the following sentence, i.e., "God, for whom Mr. Durant entertained a good humored affection, was in his heaven, and all was again well with Mr. Durant's world" (p. 35). The choice of the sensual descriptors, the word alignment, and in particular the use of the noun "cloak," provide an immediate clue to the duplicity of Mr. Durant's personality. An orderly, upright Christian husband and family man outwardly, Mr. Durant inwardly harbors lecherous longings for young girls, fantasizes flirtations, and titillates himself in his casual affair with a twenty-year-old virgin.

His mantle of respectability, as a forty-nine-year-old manager in the rubber works and a sensible father of three children, actually disguises a deep-seated abhorrence for women and a dark erotic nature.

Parker, who had not forgiven MacArthur for his abandonment and her suffering,[26] chose to portray him in this story as a contemptible middle-class monster. The depiction of Mr. Durant's cruelty to his secretary, whose abortion he will only partly pay for, (a clear echo of MacArthur's thirty dollar offer), his abuse toward his wife, and his sadistic treatment of the female dog served not only to purge Parker's personal pain, but to expose in generic terms the brutal insensitivity of male tyranny over women.[27]

Parker's language in the opening sequences that describes Mr. Durant's responses to the things about him contain passages that are shaded with innuendo. We note that Mr. Durant looked at the "rubber works," his place of business, and "nodded approvingly at the solid red pile . . . rising impressively into the darkness" (p. 35). One cannot ignore the detail of the "rubber works" as possible suggestive male slang, associated with condoms, an extension perhaps of the "cloaking" imagery of the first line. Nor can the oblique hints at male prowess in the subsequent phrasing, i.e., "the solid red pile . . . rising impressively into the darkness," be overlooked. As a satiric wit, known for her coy mastery of colloquialism,[28] Parker could not be unaware of the connotative impact in the deliberate choice of the "rubber works," as Mr. Durant's place of business.

The force of the sexually suggestive language strikes the reader further as Mr. Durant goes on to rhapsodize that at the rubber works, "you would go far" (p. 35), that you could not find a more "up and coming outfit" (p. 35), and there "welled" in him a "pleasing, proprietary sense of being a part of it" (p. 35).

Mr. Durant further observes with particular delight that he pursues a path on Center Street that is "wet" and "dented," spotted with "thick puddles," which "fed his pleasure" (p. 35) and add to the reader's growing impression of his sensually responsive nature.

He regards his "sharp interest" (p. 35) in the shapely young girl who stood near him at Center Street as healthy and responds by pointing his tongue and moving it "delicately along his cool, smooth upper lip" (p. 35). In addition to the attention that her tight little skirt and pretty thin legs command from him, more importantly, Mr. Durant notes a run in one of her stockings that provoked in him an "odd desire to catch his thumbnail in the present end of the run, and to draw it" (p. 36) to her shoe.

Thus these entries from Mr. Durant's secret thoughts portray vivid sexual fantasies tinged with a sadistic capacity to inflict cruelty and pain. The amorous inventions that Mr. Durant enacts also include the lecherous voyeurism of two nubile little neighbors girls. Mr. Durant often lingered so that he could see them "run up the steps," their narrow skirts sliding "up over their legs" (p. 42), an image, on this particular day, linked to the girl with the run in her stocking.

During the ride home on the streetcar, we learn of the actual affair with Rose and more of the inner scaffolding of Mr. Durant's attitudes toward women. He was charmed, we find out, with the idea that he was the first man in Rose's life, an idea he later came to regard as manipulation on her part. Virginity, is of course, a feminine virtue invented by patriarchal etiology as an ideal over which men assume they have dominion. The affair had been managed easily for three months, in the office, after hours, with the lights out, behind locked doors. Rose made no demands on him, never thought of stirring up marital troubles for him. It was for him a "restful" entanglement that she spoiled by getting "in trouble" (p. 39), as she finally blurted out, a phrase they both referred to, even in their private thoughts, to describe her condition.

This semantic detail serves to reflect a great deal about Mr. Durant's patriarchal views, and provides insights into Parker's sense of prescribed female roles. The reader can construct an authorial intention that censures Mr. Durant's contemptuous indifference toward Rose as he refuses to take on responsibility for his sexual acts. "In trouble," with its pejorative inference, translates as the exclusive domain of the woman's world, i.e., the female bungler who has somehow messed things up and spoiled everything by stupidly impregnating herself with male sperm.

We remember that Parker thought of her untimely pregnancy as a "mess," and punished herself for having done something wicked in both bearing and aborting the pregnancy. She apparently attempted a self-inflicting barb when she remarked to Benchley after the abortion, "Serves me bloody right, for putting all my eggs in one bastard."[29] The abortion was destined to become a subject for laughter, but Parker's fictionalized version of herself as the ruined little secretary, exploited by a rapacious boss and traumatized by unrequited love, was far from comic relief.

As the prototype for Mr. Durant, Charles MacArthur epitomized in his lack of responsibility toward Parker and his unfeelingness for her plight, the egocentricity of male cultural mythologies. Rose, the mistress in the story, is demeaned and debased for ambitious sexuality and violations of social taboos. She alone, not Mr. Durant her lover, is regarded as the outcast, and her tribulations are appraised by him as the deserving sinful catastrophe of a fallen woman.[30] The sexual trespass that produced her degrading fall has cost her the right to respectability. She is the true sinner; the unwed pregnancy, not the adultery that produced it, is the true sin.

In order to conform to male mythologies, Rose blocks the meaning by "telling it slant,"[31] a necessary indirection in a patriarchal order. The society of the 1920s enforced this deception for women. Rose sacrifices the validity of her actual experience, i.e., being pregnant, and names her truth in an alien language more suitable to the dominant group. By whose standards is she "in trouble"? Does pregnancy always imply trouble or only under certain conditions? Why is Rose in trouble and not Mr. Durant?

According to James Britton, "the objects and events of the world do not present themselves to us ready classified. The categories into which they are divided are the categories into which we divide them."[32] But who is the we?

It is men who have made the world that women inhabit, and men who define it. Hence the language that Rose uses determines her reality in the male-identified world of Mr. Durant's creation. Parker, sharply attuned to the colloquialisms of her day, reported to Marion Capron "that her stories make themselves stories by telling themselves through what people say."[33] Thus, gender-determined phrasing functions as in integral facet of this intention.

To this end, Mrs. Durant, like Rose, who speaks briefly in the story, presents a similar sampling of female deference in language. Mrs. Durant expresses herself a total of four times in the story. In three instances, her statements are abruptly cut off by Mr. Durant, severed by use of a dash, obfuscating her attempt to establish a serious position. In the fourth instance, she is permitted three words of nervous submission.

Taken collectively, Mrs. Durant's four segments of dialogue show the following syntactic patterns, under the designated headings.

In referring to the care of the dog
"There now—didn't I tell you what a dear, good father you had? . . . That's fine, Father. With that big yard and all, I think we'll make out all right. She really seems to be an awfully good little—" (p. 44)

In acknowledging the female gender of the dog
"Well—" she began, as if about to plunge into a recital of extenuating circumstances. "Well—yes," she concluded. (p. 44)

*In attempting to dispel the corruptive effects of the dog's pregnancy on
the children*
"Well, but, Father—" began Mrs. Durant, her hands again going
off into their convulsions. "Disgusting," he repeated. (p. 46)

"But the children," she said. "They'll be just simply—" (p. 46)

The reader notes the script the author makes available to
Mrs. Durant. As both woman and wife, Mrs. Durant is allotted
little power to assert herself in the world of masculine activity
and decisiveness. Each of her statements is studded with apology and tentativeness, expressing either uncertainty, e.g., "Well,"
"but," or the mitigating effects of verbs like "think," or "seems,"
as well as empty adverbs like "really," "awfully," and "simply"
all of which express cognitive uncertainty. The speaker appears
unsure of the correctness of her statements.

In a sense, Mrs. Durant has, by virtue of her response,
opted out of any decision making. Her deferential language
not only relinquishes any authority she might claim in this situation, but also serves to disguise her own deeper levels of dependency and submissiveness in their family. Her final statement, "Well, but, Father—" and "But the children . . . They'll
just simply—" approach the convention of a child's whining and
begging. As a traditional woman, she adopts a "hyper-polite"
form of expected deference, a type of linguistic
nonresponsibility, hiding her resentment behind a show of com-
promise and childlike accommodation.

The use of nonresponsibility in these language traits implies that the wife's role is trivial. Manifested linguistically, the
subtle disparagement of sex-roles attributes nonresponsibility
as natural to Mrs. Durant, who presumably is never allowed to
become responsible in the first place, since as a woman she is
assumed to be unworthy or unable to make correct decisions.
Portrayed as indecisive and pathetic, Mrs. Durant reflects a
form of learned helplessness, the result of the patriarchal nature of authoritarian institutions.

Nowhere is this effect demonstrated more clearly than in
the final "patting" gesture of Mr. Durant, on his wife's shoulder, "in its crapy-smelling black silk" (p. 46). Just as earlier Mr.
Durant forced himself to "pat" (p. 41) Rose's thin back, as he
callously sent her off, and later he "patted the dog graciously"

(p. 42), so he finally "pats," his wife's shoulder in "its crapy-smelling black silk" (p. 46). Mr. Durant, by similarly patronizing every female in the story he condescends to touch, insults and denigrates women, though his gestures are disguised by a self-styled sense of propriety and morality. Parker's choice of the metaphoric "crapy-smelling black silk," with its phonological inferences and derogatory innuendo, is sufficient to suggest a triadic relationship between Rose, the dog, and the wife.

Parker's use of naming conventions in this story emphasizes another aspect of the sexual dimensions of women's roles as she perceives them. The connotative effect of the names "Rose" and "Ruby," who both work in the rubberworks, becomes evident. As sexual objects, linked with Mr. Durant's passion and lust, they are not only referred to by the more intimate first name, while Mr. Durant maintains his formidable surname, but they are also joined by the nameless female dog, "the woman," the anonymous code-name of the person who handles the abortion, and "Fan," the diminutive nickname of Mr. Durant's wife. "Fan," Mr. Durant's corruption of the given name "Fanny," a banal colloquial expression with exclusive female implications, consigns the wife to the same sexual reference points as the other females in the story.

Though it may be argued that the names of endearment promote intimacy and informality, this is true only if they are used by all the participants in an interaction equally. Diminutives can have subtle psychological effects on both their possessors and their users.[34] In an insidious way, a nonreciprocal situation is set up in which the women of the story ultimately lose prominence and are relegated to inferiority.

It therefore comes as no surprise, that Mr. Durant subsequently characterizes the forecasted pregnancy of the dog as "disgusting" to his wife, dreadful for the children to witness, in another linguistic act of supremacy and male meanings.

The detail of the female dog is worth examining. Dogs held special meaning for Parker. Many of her friends believed that she reserved her greatest sensitivity and only real generosity of feelings for dogs and other animals. George S. Kaufman observed, "She couldn't come to terms with any real sort of love; her only loves were her fantasies and animals—and neither could talk back . . . she was as deadly as an asp."[35] Interestingly, it was the presence of her two dogs, Woodrow Wilson and Onan, that provided Parker some meager companionship when she returned home alone after the abortion. She kept dogs most of her life, though they were often spoiled and left untrained. If Parker possessed any maternal instinct, it was demonstrated in the affection she showed her dogs. Indeed, it was well known she regarded her dogs as her only "children." Hence, the metaphoric link to the female dog and its potential motherhood is tied to relatively rare images of nurturing that were detectable in Parker's own experience.

As cited earlier, Mr. Durant's denigrating portrayal of pregnancy and birth is momentarily challenged by the wife's tentative remark, "But the children," she said, "they'll be just simply—" (p. 46). Parker's stylistic use of the dash denotes not only verbal and syntactic incompletion but, quite visually, depicts unfulfilled linguistic force. Her words are denied importance, hence they are dashed away and omitted. Like Mrs. Durant herself, they have no significant place in the text. The wife literally incarnates an underscored blank space in her alignment to her husband. Silenced and muted, Mrs. Durant is unable to state a woman's view in a way that is consistent with a woman's experience, just as Rose is similarly unable to state the condition of her pregnancy authentically.

The wife retreats into invisibility and silent acquiescence, literally under the hold of her husband. "His arm was still about his wife's shoulder as they went into dinner" (p. 46). The reader leaves Mr. Durant, as he reflects smugly on the possibility of a "fresh" start; a replacement no doubt for the sullied and deflowered Rose and a change from the stale and doggedly obedient wife, in the "crapy smelling" blouse.

Parker returns in the closing scene, to the cloaking imagery of the opening lines. Mr. Durant's mind "wrapped itself" in the knowledge that everything was all fixed. As in the beginning, Mr. Durant disguises authentic reality in a pompous pretext of decorous behavior.

Mr. Durant's view of women draws together a good deal of the male moral and social bias of his day. We understand that Parker's portrayal of Durant serves to expose his misogynistic views, which appear objectionable to the reader and which Parker inferentially also condemns.

Blatantly guilty of egregious acts of insensitivity toward woman, Mr. Durant epitomizes manhood in terms of physical prowess, sexually seducing and disparaging women both in fact and in fantasy. His life reeks with lust and lechery. In her depiction of Mr. Durant, Parker excoriates the male power drive that sanctions conquest as a form of mastery, even in domestic conflict. As a treatment of the experiences of women, the story, illuminates the baleful reality of women characters as the disadvantaged group, both in and out of the household, and by implication indicts those male traditions which overtly or covertly abuse them as females.

The historical context of Parker's life continues to be relevant at this time. Like Rose, her fictional counterpart, Parker had experienced the full effect of male abuse and rejection. Unlike Rose, she did not shamefully disappear and promise not to return.

While maintaining her celebrated facade of salty humor following the abortion, Parker nevertheless continued to be privately obsessed with her own destruction. She researched newspaper accounts of suicides, scoured undertaker's magazines, and began to wear perfume with the scent of tuberoses, the scent used for corpses. In January, after struggling through a bleak holiday, drinking and sleeping inordinately, accompanied only by the unhousebroken dogs in her apartment, Parker went into the bathroom and, with a razor Eddie had left behind some six months before, she slashed both her wrists. A restaurant delivery boy, from the Alps restaurant downstairs, found her lying unconscious on the bathroom floor.

Forty-eight hours later, in the hospital, she received her Round Table friends with a barrage of amusing banter. She had tied gay blue ribbons over the bandages on her wrists, and fluttered them about like bracelets, claiming that she had given her address as Bedpan Alley. "Eddie didn't even keep his razors sharp,"[36] she mordantly joked to Benchley. Benchley, searching for an appropriate retort, gently admonished Dorothy. "Snap out of it," he said. "You might as well live."[37] It was a remark she never forgot. Later she used it, and the occasion of her abortive suicide attempt, for one of her most bitterly sardonic and self-revealing poems, "Resume":

> Razors pain you;
> Rivers are damp;
> Acids stain you;
> And drugs cause cramp.
> Guns aren't lawful;
> Nooses give;
> Gas smells awful;
> You might as well live.[38]

At home she kept up the sham of invulnerability, decorating her bandaged wrists with black velvet ribbons and oversized bows. Eddie returned briefly and left quietly. Though the scars on her wrists healed, despair over broken love affairs would repeatedly drive her to self-punishment. Later, as in the case of "Mr. Durant," she conveyed her buried pain into fictional transformations about women, using, as Kinney suggests, "the bad times as material for writing during the good times."[39]

Fathers and Females: "The Wonderful Old Gentleman" (1926)

"All those writers who talk about their childhood," Parker said bitterly to Marion Capron. "Gentle God, if I ever wrote about mine you wouldn't sit in the same room with me."[40] Though it is true that Parker almost never spoke of her childhood, one is reluctant to believe she did not find a way to write about it, using her humor as a defense against her pain. Certainly the hatred of patriarchal values, the portrait of the old father as a sanctimonious tyrant, the aloofness of the siblings and the parasitic nature of the family, seething beneath the satiric surface of "The Wonderful Old Gentleman," owes much of its flavor to the attitudes of cynicism and acrimony originating in Parker's own family ancestry.

In "The Wonderful Old Gentleman,"[41] Dorothy Parker probes the multiple relationships and roles within a family by examining the effects of an old man's imminent death upon his heirs. It is a story that reverberates with irony and betrayal. The mantle of respectability and loyalty evoked in the title masks abusiveness and hypocrisy. The mood is somber and vaguely sadistic.

Apparently, sometime in 1925, it was Parker's original idea to write a novel about her family. She intended to draw on two themes; her father's second marriage to Eleanor Lewis, and the final years surrounding her father's death. She began the work while living for the summer on a farm in Stamford, Connecticut with Deems Taylor while his wife Mary was in Europe. Taylor was part of the "extended" family of the Round Table, but was also at this time romantically linked to Dorothy in the familiar pattern of doomed and messy love affairs that were to mark Dorothy's life.

The novel was a painful undertaking that remained unfinished, but out of the effort came the piece she entitled "The Wonderful Old Gentleman," with the pungent subtitle, "A Story Proving That No One Can Hate Like a Close Relative." The subtitle has never appeared in publication. The characters in the story are thinly veiled disguises of family members: her sister and older brother, and perhaps even herself in the vicious daughter. Though she added twenty years to her father's age and made him eighty-four at his death, the depiction of the old gentleman as selfish and exploitive was intentional.

While the old man lies dying upstairs in the shabby and squalid house of Allie Bain, the timid daughter, Hattie Whittaker, the wealthy pompous daughter, who had no place for her father, but found a place for his worldly possessions, affirms her aristocratic presence and haughty dominance as manipulator of the family.

The story opens with a detailed description of the Bain's home. The living room, the furniture, the ornaments suggest the barrenness of their existence, likening the interior of the room to a "home chamber of horrors, modified a bit for family use" (p. 52).

As the two sisters and the son-in-law converse, sharing a vigil at the deathbed of the "wonderful old gentleman," the differences in their responses to the father's life and anticipated death emerge.

Allie Bain, exploited and ignored, accepts both the humble plight of her life as well as the manipulation of her wealthy sister, Hattie. Hattie, an opinionated and self-centered schemer, has arranged for the father to live with the poorer Bains rather than with her own family. In addition, she has persuaded the father to leave her his entire estate.

As the conversation turns to reminiscence over family history, intended to praise the old man's will and alertness, the mean-spirited side of the old gentleman is unwittingly revealed. When the father dies that evening, Mrs. Bain immediately collapses in passionate weeping, while Mrs. Whittaker in a statement shaded with irony pronounces her father's demise "a lovely death" (p. 64).

The jaundiced eye that Parker cast on the family, particularly on male patriarchal tradition, was clearly traceable to her own history. We know that Parker's family life was filled with bitterness. Her mother, Eliza, a Scotswoman, died during Dorothy's infancy. Dorothy was terrified of her father, a Jew named Rothschild, whom she could not speak of without horror. She could never bring herself to call the second Mrs. Rothschild, a pious eccentric, anything but "the housekeeper," even in adulthood. She almost never referred to her family in later life, and when she did, it was with loathing. According to Kinney, Parker never accepted her mixed parentage and professed wanting to write an autobiography for the express purpose of calling it *Mongrel*.[42]

Parker's revulsion for her father came quite literally from the fact that he was living testimony to her Jewishness, an embarrassment she could not endure. Even as a child, she fantasized being Catholic rather than Jewish. Somehow she believed that no "thoroughbred" could be Jewish. Rothschild's name, appearance, and behavior, despite his unrelenting pursuit of respectability, signaled to the entire world the humiliating fact that Dorothy was a Jew. Talmudic law, by which the mother, not the father, determines the Jewishness of the child, did little in the eyes of Dorothy to extricate her from this perpetual indignity.

The second Mrs. Rothschild, a Christian schoolteacher like the first, set upon a zealous course of moral and religious instruction to save Dorothy's soul. Dorothy was enrolled in New York's Blessed Sacrament Convent, where the strict disciplines of Catholic schooling were legendary, and Dorothy's long anticipated dream to be "Catholicized" were incarnated into an intolerable nightmare. The school ultimately could not restrain Dorothy's irreverent and rebellious nature. It is alleged that in one well-known incident, Dorothy referred to the "Immaculate Conception" as "spontaneous combustion," and eventually her devilish behavior and caustic humor drove the nuns to distraction.

To the displeasure of her father, Dorothy's family was advised to "find a more suitable educational establishment."[43] At home, Dorothy was required to pay a form of penance; a regimen of discipline, early meals, and long periods alone were strictly enforced by her didactic father. These early associations with patriarchal authority, dreaded and disturbing, were later recalled with abhorrence. She did not please her father and her father did not please her.

Dorothy developed little love or even understanding of family, a view clearly generated in this story. Her fictional writings seldom portray compassion within families and are almost devoid of loving mothers and fathers.

The gallery of her fictional characters is universally lacking in filial warmth; likewise in her personal life, Dorothy intentionally characterized herself as a rejected outsider. Her mother, Eliza, she was convinced had betrayed her by dying young; her relationship with her stepmother, Eleanor, became so hostile and sullen that she often wished the woman dead. Mrs. Rothschild became increasingly frustrated with Dorothy, and the gap between them widened. When Eleanor did die suddenly in 1903, Dorothy felt the weight of it on her conscience. Now twice traumatized by maternal loss, she responded by developing the conviction that she deserved punishment. She internalized the death of Eliza as a wicked mental murder, the evil fulfillment of her darkest desires, and a source of the negativity and disdain which was to manifest itself later so piercingly in her astringent humor.

Within the family she believed she was treated like an afterthought, the last child of an indifferent household that showed no loved for her. John Keats alleges:

> "It was quite a childhood: a terrifying father hammering her wrists; a rather lunatic stepmother hammering at her mind; a sister and a brother too remote in age for any communion; the servant put out of reach by social convention . . . She hated being a Jew and began to think that her mother had deserted her by dying. She began to hate herself."[44]

Despite this bitter portrait, which has been affirmed by biographers and embellished by Parker herself, there appears to have been a generous, emotional, and playfully teasing side to Henry Rothschild, and a degree of love and laughter in the house that Dorothy purposely chose to ignore. New biographical research suggests, in fact, that Dorothy and Henry exchanged pleasant letters and even verse, and that Henry was more tolerant of her behavior than Dorothy allowed.[45]

Nevertheless, in Dorothy's version of her reality she preferred to depict herself as a deprived child, an innocent victim of a heartless father, a wicked stepmother, and a dysfunctional family. She loved to fantasize herself as an unloved orphan—her favorite role—a romance that nurtured her cynical view and black humor, but simultaneously fed the gnawing emptiness and depression of her adult life.

For whatever reasons, one thing emerges from the writings and confessionals; Dorothy regarded her father as a bully, a hypocrite, and an enemy. According to Leslie Frewin, when Parker received the news that her father had died, it was of sufficient unimportance to her that she did not even attend his funeral.[46]

Parker's ascent to adulthood amidst a turbulent family, her bitter memories of a deceased mother, a truculent father and a religiously fanatic stepmother, all of which helped shape her attitudes probably most of her life, nourished the unhappy wit that cast into prose the strained family relationships, the contempt for men, and the ironic view of women that emerges from this story.

Parker is particularly concerned in the story with the female personality and the working out of female roles in the family cosmogony. She approaches this task in a blatant portrayal of two female stereotypes, neither of whom is either admirable or heroic. As in her own life, there was little rapport between siblings.

Allie Bain, the submissive and martyred sister, who, recalls the mythic Griselda figure,[47] is contrasted with Hattie Whittaker, the classic overbearing bitch. However, according to Suzanne Bunkers, Parker used the female stereotypes not merely as figures of ridicule, but as a form of feminist social criticism.[48]

Though the provocative rendering of the sisters as satiric stereotypes overtly dominates the pages of the story and bears close examination, it is the invisible role of the father, as male patriarch and authority figure, which provides the most essential link to the separate and mutual development of these women.

We come to know the father from snatches of conservation among his heirs and from his material contribution to the room. We are warned from the opening line that the room is a monument to squalor and discomfort. "The furniture was dark and cumbersome" (p. 52). The paper was the color of stale mustard, and the ornaments and statuary suggested eternal struggle and pain. Even the religious art was devoted to "agonized eyes" and "bitter tears" (p. 53). However, buried in the memorabilia are two contributions from the old gentleman that provide insight into his cruel and callous nature.

"Beneath the windows hung a painting in oil of two lost sheep, huddled hopelessly together in the midst of a wild blizzard" (p. 53). In addition to this gift from the old gentleman, we are told of his wedding gift, "a savage china kitten eternally about to pounce upon a plump and helpless mouse" (p. 54). From these artifacts, we deduce our first clues. The father's insensitivity and cruelty toward others belie his reputation as the wonderful old gentleman.

The two lost sheep huddled against the blizzard, becomes a more profound image, when we learn that Matt, the old man's son, whose docility Allie shared, was driven away by the father's unrelenting dominance. Later significantly referred to as the "black sheep of the family" (p. 61), Matt happily marries an actress, an act of independence that Hattie, like her father, regarded as hastening the old man's death. Perhaps Parker saw in this sequence an echo to her own treatment as the free-spirited and rebellious adolescent in a disapproving patriarchal family.

We eventually learn from further conversation that the old man has also driven away his grandson, Paul, whom he regarded as a nuisance in the house, enslaved the Bains in endless servitude and acts of obligatory but redundant duties, and willed his favoritism, in his life, and his fortune, in his death, to his wealthy, equally callous daughter, who, like him, dominates everything and everyone around her.

One small reference to the mother provides the final brush-stroke in the portrait of the old tyrant. Mrs. Bain remembers the mother, begging the children to try and keep "father in a good humor" no matter what, often cheating at cards herself "so as to be sure and not win from him" (p. 63), in order to escape his fury.

Parker's authorial stance on the woman issue in this story involves not merely a mocking satire of two sisters caught in an amusing antithetical relationship, but more profoundly exposes the damaging effects of a male-dominated household, tyrannized by a traditional patriarch who ultimately prescribes a society in his own image.

In Parker's life, her father exercised a similar narrow-minded insensitivity over the household. According to one especially painful memory, Henry's idea of family "treats" were routine Sunday excursions to Woodlawn Cemetery to visit Dorothy's mother's grave. She remembers him wailing, "We're all here, Eliza! I'm here. Dottie's here. Mrs. Rothschild is here." Marion Meade claims that "At these moments Dorothy hated him."[49]

The author, by implication, asks us to condemn both the prolonged martyrdom that has enervated Allie, as well as the predatory self-indulgence that has energized Hattie. The portrayal of the two sisters, at either end of the female spectrum, evokes mixed reactions from the reader. Although it is Hattie Whittaker whose bitchy, scheming power intimidates the sister, and aggressively controls the outcome of events in the story, ironically, it is Allie, the passive and colorless daughter, who invites our greater interest.

Allie Bain's life has not been happy. Uncomplaining and pliant, she allows herself to be used and exploited by her father and her sister. But her passiveness and martyrdom are not as simple as they seem. From what reservoir of experiences does Allie shape her identity? Is Allie's submissiveness the result only of Hattie's dominance, or does it draw from other origins?

The paucity of masculine affirmation in Allie's life is directly linked to her own self-image. Beginning with the father, Allie learns early, as did her dutiful mother, to placate, accommodate and submit.

While Allie's slavish servitude to her father was expected, even abused, Hattie's polite gestures of filial interest in him were prized and rewarded with affection.

> She came to see him several times a month, bringing him jelly
> or potted hyacinths. Sometimes she sent her car and chauffeur
> for him, so that he might take an easy drive through the town,
> and Mrs. Bain might be afforded a chance to drop her cooking
> and accompany him. (p. 57).

He took pride in her, and relished being told that she was like
him. Her wealth was regarded as power. Her pretentious charm
was lauded.

False, perfunctory emotions were not only excused but
actually encouraged. Though her manner was offensive and
her behavior artificial, it was plain that Hattie was the favored
daughter. Gracious, attractive, well-married, meticulously
groomed, Hattie incarnated the "lady-like" qualities and deco-
rum, both as a woman and as a daughter, esteemed by the old
gentleman's polite paternalistic world of values; "her bearing
had always that calm that only the correctly attired may enjoy"
(p. 55). It comes as no surprise that the word "lady" figured
prominently in her conversation.

In a profound sense, Hattie's charm and influence with
her father is the result of a value system derived from the myth
and lore of a male-dominated tradition which places a high priority on conventional "female" attributes. "In this hierarchy,
beauty, charm, grace, personal attractiveness are purported to
engender male affection."[50] And, as de Beauvoir suggests, if
the father shows affection for his daughter, as the old gentleman has toward Hattie, she feels that her existence is splen-
didly justified; she is enshrined with all the virtues that others
have to acquire with difficulty. As a result, she is fulfilled and
idealized.

Allie, on the other hand, in her rumpled white shirtwaist
and old blue kitchen skirt, was the quintessence of disarray and
distraught untidiness. In contrast to Hattie's stylishness, Allie's
plainness is striking, "straggling hair, gray at the front, with
strands of almost lime color in the little twist at the back" (p.
56). Predictably, the father is contemptuous of Allie's unsight-
liness and poverty, regarding them as symbols of failure and
weakness. Unable to fulfill the supreme necessity as a daughter, i.e., to charm her father's heart, Allie's devotion, despite
its zeal and intensity, is unrewarded. The old gentleman with-
holds his love and schedules Allie to a lifelong sentence of his
disdain.[51]

Hattie was a "fine woman—a fine woman" (p. 58), he was fond of saying, but he used to "raise Cain when Allie didn't cut up his meat fast enough to suit him" (p. 59). The literal reference to "Cain," the original defiler of family, combined with the image of the father's rapacious and carnivorous appetite, links the old man to a potent source of malevolence.

We have only to review the various contexts in which the sisters are nurtured by the patriarchal old man, to understand the distinctions in their personalities. It need not astonish us that while her sister plays the imperious "Bitch," Allie plays the servile "Griselda."[52]

Despite the pathetic nature of Allie's character, the author is not unsympathetic with the fragility of humans such as she, assaulted as they often are by the callous and self-serving malefactors of the world. Allie's psyche, battered and beaten by years of low esteem and the denial of self-worth, is a product of the impoverished nature of her environment. In this sense, buried in the walls of her tomb-like home lies the key to her mental and emotional state.

For entry into the inner workings of Allie Bain's psyche, we are led back to the living room for a guided tour of Allie's undisguised self.

Parker devotes the first two and a half pages of the story to a plethora of details that characterize the gruesome interior of the Bain's living room.

> If the Bains had striven for years, they could have been no more successful in making their living room into a small but admirably complete museum of objects suggesting strain, discomfort, or the tomb. (p. 52)

So the story begins. The reader is struck immediately by the recurring and persistent references to objects and artifacts that reflect pain. One might catalogue as follows: The furniture was subject to "painful creaking" (p. 52), when it could bear no more; the center table was upheld by the arms of three carved naked female figures, that "perpetually strained" (p. 53); the books were held by bookends kept in place by the "straining shoulder-muscles of two bronze-colored plaster elephants" (p. 53). On the mantle the figure of a peasant boy in the act of removing a thorn from his foot was in "cruel pain," and the chariot drivers above him lashed their horses till "their hearts burst, and they dropped in their traces" (p. 53). The religious art reeked of "ghastly detail" of the Crucifixion, and the two paintings, one from the father and one from the husband, depicted scenes, respectively, of the hopelessly "lost sheep," discussed earlier, and a "red automobile trying to dash across the train track before the iron terror shattered" (p. 53) it. The ornament of the "savage china kitten about to pounce on the mouse" (p. 54), mentioned previously, and the ashtrays of "grotesque heads tufted with bits of grey human hair, and given bulging, dead, glass eyes and mouths" (p. 54), to receive their waste, complete the collection of incarnated misery. What are we to make of this litany of pain?

Certainly the objects themselves are rife with hints of suffering that relate to Allie's life. Based on Jung's notion of sexual allegory,[53] the room may be regarded as an important female symbol, emblematic of the womb, or passage way. Allie Bain, then, as her full name implies, connotes associations with narrow corridors or alleys of pain; while her last name alone evokes the parallel to "bane," as in that which ruins or spoils. We further recall that some of the articles in the room were wedding presents and gifts from both her father and husband. The researcher is urged to follow the suggestiveness of the language, coupled with the references to marriage, husband, and father in this morbid setting, as reflective of the failure of Allie Bain's life as a woman. Just as the paper on the wall had faded into the stale yellow color of mustard, a reflection of Allie's emotional torpor,[54] and the pattern melted into hordes of tortured profiles, for those eyes "sensitive" (p. 52) enough to perceive it, so Allie Bain's life as a woman dissolved into a similar agony.

Parker encoded Allie's pain into the objects of her own living room. The creaking of the furniture that seemed to be "wrung from its brave silence when it could bear no more," has a recapitulation of childbirth imagery and labor pains. We note, by contrast, that Hattie had no children. "The earthy smell" and "furry dust in the crevice" is susceptible of more than one interpretation. The table, located significantly at the center, upheld by the strained arms of three naked females, which supported the bookends of straining elephants, reverberates with Mrs. Bain's struggle to hold things together against the bullishness of her father and the vicissitudes of her life. The young boy in the act of removing a painful "thorn" (p. 53) from his foot remains fixed on the mantle, while the Bains' young son, Paul, regarded as a nuisance to his grandfather, was driven away. Even the horses, whipped ferociously by their driver until they drop of exhaustion, call to mind the Bains' tireless effort to please the father.

The watercolor copy of "a Mother of Sorrows" (p. 53), and the ghastly details of the martyrdom of Saint Sebastian, cutting the "soft-looking body" (p.53), cannot be ignored in their indirect associations with Allie's deadening life of sacrifice and service.

Finally the author compels our attention to the grotesque painting of a train, about to shatter a small red car. The depiction was so frightening that "nervous visitors who were given chairs facing this scene usually made opportunity to change their seats" (p. 53). The painting, we recall, was a gift from her husband. Given the psychoanalytic associations of trains with sexual drive and phallic energy,[55] what might this artifact cryptically portray about Allie's marriage? If, as Jung suggests, a rushing train often connotes male sexual power, symbolically expressed, then the husband's choice of the painting and subsequent gift to his wife Allie, reflects, unconsciously perhaps, an essentially masculine attitude in his relationship to Allie, one that appears to embody some aspect of dominant and/or aggressive sexuality. Furthermore, the wedding gift from the father depicting the savage attack on a "helpless mouse" (p. 54) carries a sadistic message of its own. The ferocious nature of the father appears ironically portrayed in the statue as the rapacious cat, eternally about to pounce on its victim. As a wedding gift to the daughter Allie, the ornament is a further emblem of male attitudes toward women.

Although Emily Toth claims that "The Wonderful Old Gentleman" provides comic opportunities for ironic laughter at human frailties, focusing on "the peculiarities of the Good Souls, not on the victimization of the truly good,"[56] her analysis seems to ignore the overwhelming evidence of authentic pain carefully detailed in the story.

While Allie's pain and personal failure as a woman are reflected in the deadness of her environment, there is one moment when Allie Bain comes to life. At the announcement of the old man's death, Allie collapses into "passionate weep-ing" (p. 64). We are struck by the word, "passionate," an usual emotive response from a presumably passive personality. Con-sider this phrase in juxtaposition with an earlier statement, claiming that despite years of practice at crying, Allie "did not do it well" (p. 55).

Allie's ability to cry "passionately" at the moment of her father's death goes beyond cathartic release, and suggests a sensual emotional liberation, a vitality heretofore buried by her burden as the dutiful daughter.

Indeed the wish for her father's death was more than hinted at moments before, when, exhausted by the night time vigil, Allie in an unguarded moment says to her sister, "'Goodness, I had no idea it was anywhere so late. I wish—.' She stopped just in time, crimson at what her wish would have been" (p. 63). The fulfillment of her unexpressed wish was presently granted.

The final words of the nurse, spoken "earnestly" to con-sole Allie, ironically touch the mixture of guilt and relief she has repressed until now. "It's really a blessing, that's what it is" (p. 64), said Miss Chester. These words would seem an appro-priate end to the story.

However, Parker adds one more sentence—gratuitously it seems. "Among them, they got Mrs. Bain up the stairs" (p. 54). Why is this sentence necessary? Why would Allie Bain, slavish and dutiful daughter, fail to rush to the bedside of her dead father whom she had assiduously tended for five years? What is Parker suggesting about Allie's inability to climb the stairs?

The sentence is not gratuitous. The placement of the sen-tence is inferentially significant. As the two women struggle to maneuver Allie into this last gesture of servitude, her body strangely resists. The author invites the reader ultimately to reflect on Allie's psychological state, as a woman, as she senses emotional freedom and the instant of release from her patriar-chal bondage. We are drawn unequivocally to Allie's "passion-ate weeping," which momentarily paralyzes her and renders her unable and unwilling to climb the stairs alone, and face the dead object of her mingled hate and love.

It is not irrelevant to recall at this time that Parker's own loathing of her father, deserved or decreed, was sufficient to keep her from attending his funeral. Parker's hostility toward the original patriarch in her life has profound resonance in this final scene. Some years after this work appeared, in a conversation with Oscar Levant, Parker said that the reason she did not continue her brief foray into psychotherapy was because once she had told Dr. Barach, her psychiatrist, that she hated her father, she could think of nothing else to say. The weight of that statement seems self-evident.

The portrayal of the two sisters in "The Wonderful Old Gentleman" furnishes the reader with an ironic treatment of two women shaped in dichotomous but mutually flawed female roles. However, the reader may feel uneasy about the degree of irony implicit in Parker's portraiture. As role models, neither woman engenders much inspiration. The author appears to ridicule both females who are outwardly depicted as either submissively weak or assertively manipulative. Yet, despite her superiority, Hattie, like Parker herself, is still a forceful woman who knows how to get exactly what she wants. To that extent, she may evoke some positive reaction from the reader, and imply some authorial sanction, i.e., Hattie's aggressiveness vis-à-vis Allie's passiveness might be preferable. Though Hattie cannot divest herself of the false connections to her father and his paternalistic values even to the end, the reader's view of Allie may be tempered by the understanding that Allie's final action indicates an attempt to cast off the yoke of patrimony. In so doing, she faintly rebels not only against the abuses of the old gentleman, but against the legacy of those abuses mirrored in and perpetuated by her sister Hattie.

In 1926, the year "The Wonderful Old Gentleman" was published, Parker returned from her first trip to Europe to find that the old Algonquin group, in a sense, her only remaining "family," was breaking up. Within two years, she secured a divorce from Edwin Parker on the grounds of cruelty. In her relationships with men, she became more promiscuous and less discerning.

Her depression and despondency increased; her life became an orgy of excessiveness and self-indulgence. She became aggressive and hostile, especially to her friends. Warnings to the contrary, she continued to drink heavily, and attempted suicide a third time with barbiturates. Her friends had never seen her this low.

She was later to recall these days with bitter acrimony in her poem, "Rhyme Against Living":

> If wild my breast and sore my pride,
> I bask in dreams of suicide;
> If cool my heart and high my head,
> I think, "How lucky are the dead!"[57]

In a vignette that pathetically reflected her misery, Parker responded to a bartender's query, "What are you having?" "Not much fun," Parker lashed back, using her wit as her only weapon against pain. Much of that pain had its genesis in a bitter family history, recalled momentarily in the saga of disharmony and patrimony in "The Wonderful Old Gentleman."

Sexual Roles and Social Taboos: "A Telephone Call" (1928)

1928 was a fertile year for Dorothy Parker. She was leading a tumultuous social life, staying up late, drinking a lot, but nevertheless producing some of her best work. *Enough Rope,* her collection of verse published in December of 1927 made publishing history by becoming an instant best seller, an unprecedented achievement for a volume of poetry. Edmund Wilson was correct in stating that her verse was rooted in contemporary reality, reflecting a very particular time and place; the chic, fashionable, black authenticity of the Flapper Age. Its sensational reception, and smart salty humor, propelled Parker into the ranks of literary celebrity. Protestations not withstanding, she had become famous. Her work and wit were in demand. She was inundated with invitations and interviews, adored and pampered by attractive, moneyed social circles. The advantages of these friendships were undeniable, but ultimately artistically costly.

Despite missed deadlines, and a history of being perpetually late with her copy at *The New Yorker,* Parker published in "The Bookman" the comic but deadly serious monologue "A Telephone Call."[58]

Although establishing links between an artist's private life and his creative work carries its own risk, there can be no doubt that Parker could draw upon her own experience as a woman in the matter of unrequited love. In 1928, the year "A Telephone Call" was published, Dorothy Parker became entangled in an affair with John Wiley Garrett II, an investment banker, a straight-laced corporate type, a good-looking, graceful man, with a long list of female conquests and a fierce, well-known determination not to get married. A right-wing politically correct Republican who sailed, played golf and tennis, and belonged to the American Legion, he was the romantic incarnation of Parker's unrelenting quest for her handsome Gentile.

He shared none of Parker's liberal tendencies, which had recently included a highly publicized personal protest on behalf of Sacco and Vanzetti that landed her in jail for one night; nor did he seem to care for or comprehend her love of literature. Indeed, later trying to recall what they had in common, she remembered with some difficulty that he spoke about his war experiences in the Artillery and about his recollections of fraternity life at Williams College. "We were both pretty fairly tight"[59] most of the time, Parker admitted, and she retained only foggy impressions of their romantic liaison. It was clear that the combination of liquor, a romantic imagination, and the Roman numeral II following his name, (as she once had fantasized with Edwin Pond Parker II) was sufficient to transform Garrett into an alluring lover. In reality, he was appallingly dull; they had nothing in common and their affair was destined for disaster and heartbreak.

His faithlessness, and especially his habit of breaking his promises to telephone, drove her to madness. She would sit by the phone waiting and agonizing, afraid and embarrassed to phone him. It is precisely this tormented image which provides the entire scenario for her story "A Telephone Call."

As the story opens, an unnamed speaker, torn between her desire to phone the man she loves and her fear of violating the social taboo, pleads with God to let the phone ring as she simultaneously threatens to make the call herself.

The speaker addresses God throughout the sketch. She interprets the man's failure to call her as her own fault, the result of some terrible "sin" she has committed. Initially, she begs God's forgiveness, promising to repent. "I'll be good, God.

I will try to be better, I will, if You will let me see him again"
(p. 120).

Even as the speaker promises to be "better," her repressed
rage begins to emerge. First she turns her anger toward the
telephone, threatening to pull its "filthy roots off the wall"
(p. 120). Then she turns her fury on her lover, wishing she
could make him cry or "hurt him like hell" (p. 121). Nevertheless, every time she threatens to act, she subsequently relents.
With a cringing feeling of helplessness, the speaker pendulates
between penitence and fury, marshalling invectives against
men, God, and the telephone, while seeking the Lord's
mercy, as the evening passes uninterrupted by her lover's
call.

In the end, tortured by the intensity of her conflicting
feelings, the speaker pathetically appeals to God's pity once
again, beseeching him to let the telephone ring instantly, de-
claring that if he hasn't called by the time she counts "five hun-
dred by fives" (p. 124) she will call him herself.

Her struggle remains unresolved. Though determined to
make the crucial call, the story ends as the speaker begins the
agonizing and paralyzing count, "five, ten, fifteen" (p. 124).

One of Parker's most celebrated monologues, the story
begins structurally with a plea that appears innocent and familiar enough. "Please, God, let him telephone me" (p. 119). The
narrator's continued entreaties to God form the core of a stylistic device that hinges on satire, exaggeration, and repetition
for comic effect. The story as traditionally read is a conventional, humorous monologue. The plight of the narrator and
her mounting anxiety as she awaits the crucial phone call provide both amusement and pleasure for readers who regard her
antics as asinine and silly or identify with the comic familiarity
of her behavior.

On the surface, the contradictions between the triviality
of the situation and the intensity of the narrator create an ostensibly funny situation. But the story is far from a burlesque.
On a deeper level, the humor serves to mask the humiliation
and confusion that the speaker feels as a woman.

> Dear God, let him call me now. I won't ask anything else of You,
> truly I won't. It isn't very much to ask. It would be so little, to You.
> God, such a little, little thing. (p. 119)

These opening lines quickly establish the traditional sexual roles, i.e, the unnamed female speaker acknowledging the dominance of male initiative with the line, "let *him* telephone *me* now" (emphasis added). The entire monologue is structured as a female response to the demands of a male-identified social context; the speaker's passivity, accommodation, and frustration are the expected characteristics of her role.

In the monologue itself, the verbal structure employs a form of double voice and verbal subversion. The speaker presents herself on various levels: a public, pleasing, feminine self, "I would be sweet . . . I would be gay," for example, juxtaposed with a mocking, subversive, private voice of discontent, "I wish to God I could make him cry" (p. 121), the voice of introspection. Malice and savagery are masked with wit. The reader finds the story ostensibly funny because the full range of contradictions in persona as the speaker shifts her language. She begins:

> Please, God, let him telephone me now. Dear God, let him call me now. I won't ask anything else of You, truly I won't. It isn't very much to ask. It would be so little, to You. God, such a little, little, thing. (p. 119)

As the language intensifies and becomes more colored with slang and colloquialism, the personality revealed appears more violent:

> Why can't that telephone ring? Why can't it? Couldn't you ring? Ah, please, couldn't you? You dammed ugly, shiny thing. Damn you. I'll pull your filthy roots out of the wall. I'll smash your smug black face in little bits. Damn you to hell. (p. 120)

The woman's personality here is divided, and the contradictory nature of her language functions as a vehicle of personality as well as thought. As the narrator's linguistic behavior alternates, she tells us not only about the world, but also, through the form and content of her language patterns, a great deal about herself.

The question of the narrator's identity brings us to the consideration of sexually distinct language patterns in the story that also shape personal and social identity. For example, the speaker herself refers to the fact that she is a "girl" (p. 120) whom a young "man" (p. 121) says he'll call up. The substitution of "girl" for "woman" while the lover is referred to as "man" rather than "boy" suggests the sex distinctions in language, both self-imposed and socially ordained, that subsequently determine male and female differences in roles.[60] The speaker's identity here is characterized by her immaturity and frivolousness as a "girl" not to be entrusted with decisions of any serious nature. Appealing to a woman's vanity about her youth, her childishness, and her appearance, the woman is furthermore relegated to a position of social existence, which is defined linguistically by others, in this case, the dominant gender.[61]

The image of the God to whom the narrator incessantly pleads carries particular impact and invites further examination of the story with regard to language behavior and social commentary. In light of the feminist argument that man has created a male God who in both daily worship and prayer is portrayed in masculine terms, women are not only denied the image encompassed by God, but more importantly are depicted as dangerous and branded as the source of evil in the myth of the Fall, a "cosmic falsenaming,"[62] metamorphisizing the male viewpoint into God's viewpoint. Conversely, the myth identifies the origins of evil in the mold of femaleness.[63]

As created and evolved by males, the myth projects guilt upon woman as the cause of the patriarchal fall, a distortion in which women become scapegoats in a patriarchal lie that ensures both their submission and their perpetual guilt. From this initial distortion of naming God as male and female as evil, a superiority-inferiority relationship has become a principle encoded both in language and social position.

How does this argument on the politics of naming impact on Parker's monologue? Not only is the language of the monologue incessantly and resonantly shaded with the supplications of a generically inferiorized woman, but the sketch etches out a class portrait of obsessive female guilt as well.

What patriarchal rules of the game has the speaker in the monologue violated that cause this guilt? It is true that the monologue pivots on the issue of social conventions between men and women in the courting process. Over and over again the protagonist debates with herself as to the advisability of calling "him." By phoning the man she loves, the speaker understands that she will trespass a social taboo. However, a closer reading of the text reveals the fact that the speaker has already violated that social taboo. She phoned her lover, earlier in the day, textually prior to the opening of the scenario of the monologue.

Bitterly she admits:

> He couldn't have minded my calling him up. I know you shouldn't keep telephoning them. I know they don't like that. When you do that, they know you're thinking about them and wanting them and that makes them hate you. (p. 119)

The effect of the pronoun switch from "he" to "them" generalizes patriarchal power into a pervasive and omnipresent force that governs behavior, determines social arrangements, and inflicts retribution to the woman in a particularly punishing way. Her life as a woman is already a reproach, but her female guilt is exacerbated by the fact that in some way she has already disturbed the proper order of things and must pay. "He couldn't have thought I was bothering him. No of course, you're not, he said" (p. 119). But her nervous recollection unmasks the danger she already suspects.

> He didn't have to say that. I didn't ask him to, truly I didn't. I'm sure I didn't. I don't think he would say he'd telephone me, and then just never do it. Please don't let him do that, God. Please don't. (p. 119)

As the speaker's uneasy insecurities multiply, her language increases in its intensity. By the end of the fourth paragraph, her pleas to God are tinged with hysteria and anger.

> Oh don't laugh, God. You see. You don't know how it feels. You're so safe, there on Your throne. . . This is suffering, God, this is bad, bad suffering. . . Oh God, in the name of Thine only beloved Son, Jesus Christ, our Lord, let him telephone me now. (p. 120)

This appeal to a patriarchal God-figure, God's only offspring, His son, Christ, underscores the accepted male tradition of mastery in the hierarchy of authority. The paternalistic ruler of the world is associated here with assertive powers that women have no share in. Indeed, a patriarchal etiology that defines a male-Father-God as the creator of all things reinforces the speaker's anxiety regarding her own incapacity for action as a woman, as well as her concession to male superiority in general.[64] It is apparent that the frantic plea to God in a personal crisis is not an exclusive female rite; a man might indeed pray to God for his woman to call him. Nevertheless, in this instance, the reading is concerned with establishing the female narrator's relationship to images of authority as she perceives them. Parker suggests that the words and actions of the speaker are a concession to the belief that the determining powers, both in society and in the universe, are traditionally male-determined.

Hence, the roots of authority to which the speaker responds asserts, after all, that if God is the sole creator of the universe and that to be God is not to be a woman, then woman is man's property and at the mercy of his earthly as well as heavenly judgment. In a reality that is mono-dimensional, where males are in control, women must seek male attention and approval in order to confirm their identity. Hence, the speaker's view of herself in "A Telephone Call" depends largely on the willingness of her male partner to acknowledge her being by virtue of a "telephone call," which according to social practice only he is allowed to make.

For the woman, this acknowledgment is confounded not only by the traditional norms of male supremacy, which disallow equal status between the sexes, but also by the effect of this struggle for male attention amongst women themselves. That is to say, while men traditionally compete for achievement and worldly approval, women traditionally compete for men and male approval.[65] Female competition for men enforces a view of the world in which males continue to be seen as superior and females continue to be seen as inferior. Accordingly, males represent the positive, while females represent the negative.

This social subordination of women is the result of a situation in which women have adapted to the wishes of men and felt as if their adaptations were true to their nature. They envision themselves as men's wishes demand of them, yielding to the suggestions of a masculine value system.

By the winter of 1928, Parker saw her affair with Garrett fading. Like the narrator of "A Telephone Call," she decided that men "hate you whenever you say anything you really think. You always have to keep playing little games." Indeed, Garrett had complained of her graphic language and possessiveness.

He forbade certain of her favorite expletives, resented her position as a literary critic, and complained that she was a bad influence on him. At the age of thirty-five, Garrett, who had never wed, was the consummate flirt, playing single, married, and divorced women off against each other with masculine relish. Egotistical and elegantly vain, he enjoyed being pursued and wooed by throngs of hopeful females. He did little to conceal his exploits from Dorothy and shamelessly continued a pattern of promiscuity and deception during their entire relationship. Dorothy found herself despondent and jealous, unable to trust him and unable to leave him. She persisted in a degrading affair that left her humiliated and helpless, betrayed by her own seemingly punishing need for an indifferent paramour.

Much of this same helplessness is specifically reflected in the language of "A Telephone Call." The cruel caricature of the female speaker in "A Telephone Call," is a paradigm for the way women respond both emotionally and linguistically to a male-defined hierarchy in which they are essentially devalued.

The narrator's lexicon in the opening passage is laced with learned feminine attributes: e. g., repetitions, "let him telephone me *now* (emphasis added); "Dear God, let him call me *now*" (emphasis added); supplications, "please, please, please"; and lady-like intensifiers, such as "truly," and "it would be such a little, little thing" (p. 119). In this same opening passage of five lines, the narrator uses the word "please" five times as she beseeches God to let him telephone her, succumbing to the masculine dualities of a male lover and a male deity. The image of the male God to whom she incessantly pleads again carries particular impact. When God is depicted as a male, the female sexual relationship to all men is thereby inferred. The injunction that "Thou shalt have no other Gods before me" takes on important sexual meaning in the context.[66]

While the preceding passage clues us in to the speaker's growing trepidations over the social improprieties in having phoned her lover at the office, the following passage provides the most penetrating explanation of the speaker's true source of guilt.

> Are you punishing me, God, because I've been bad? Are You angry with me because I did that? Oh, but, God, there are so many bad people—You could not be hard only to me. And it

wasn't very bad; it couldn't have been bad. We didn't hurt anybody, God. Things are only bad when they hurt people. We didn't
hurt one single soul; You know that. You know it wasn't bad,
don't You, God? So won't You let him telephone me now? (p.
121)

This important passage is susceptible to several interpretations. On the one hand, there is the initial suggestion that
her "badness" refers to the previously cited gesture of phoning
her lover, a boldness she currently regrets. On the other hand,
it becomes clear that this particular "badness" has other, more
serious connotations. Being "bad" for a woman has specific
implications. If we follow the details of the passage closely, the
conclusion seems clear.

"Are you angry with me because I did *that?*" (emphasis
added): If "that" refers only to the phone call, then the next
lines seem inappropriate. "There are so many bad people—You
could not be hard only to me. And it wasn't very bad; it couldn't
have been bad. *We* didn't hurt anybody, God" (emphasis added;
p. 121). Why has the speaker switched the pronouns from "I" to
"We"? Is she referring to the phone call she herself made? Once
again she follows with the sentence, "*We* didn't hurt one single
soul; You know that" (emphasis added p. 121). These two instances are the only times in the entire story that the speaker
uses "we" in reference to her collaboration with her lover.

In the next paragraph, the speaker's hysterical epiphany
provides the final clue. "It was bad. I knew it was bad. All right,
God, send me to hell" (p.121). The "it," we may now conclude,
is sexual intercourse and the speaker awaits her damnation.

The mood alternations, the explosions of guilt and anger,
the psychic punishment the speaker experiences are the result
of her violations not only of social taboos but of sexual taboos
as well. Her "punishment," which she fully anticipates from
the opening moments of the story, is the purgatory of the sullied female, the just deserts of the sexually active woman in a
world of double standards. She knows she has been "bad" in
the only ways that a woman can truly be bad according to traditional social expectations. Hence, her guilt emanates from
the awareness of her own wickedness not only in her improper
social behavior, but in her "permissive," and hence promiscuous, sexual behavior. The lapse from the "he" to the "we" confirms her anxieties and self-recrimination over the affair.

I'll be so sweet to him, if he calls me. If he says he can't see me
tonight, I'll say, "Why that's all right, dear." . . . I'll be the way I
was when I first met him. Then maybe he'll like me again. . .Oh,
it's so easy to be sweet to people before you love them. (p. 121)

The narrator couples the lament of her submissiveness
with the promise to repeat its cycle of accommodation, bond-
ing herself to her oppression as she vows: "I'll be so sweet to
him. . .then maybe he'll like me again" (p.121). In so doing,
she discounts authentic love as a viable or desirable possibility
for women. She exists as the object of his needs. The myths
and taboos that have given form to cultural images of woman
as the subordinate group justify her lover's antipathy. Included
in these male "antipathies" are the notions that human experience has essentially meant the masculine experience, and thus
feminine experience has only been defined in terms of man's
subjective ideas about women.[67]

Leonore Weitzman, in her review of sex-role studies, states
that the socialization process that has shaped the sex roles individuals have come to assume characterize women as "passive,
dependent, and emotional," and men as "aggressive, active, and
instrumental."[68] While these adjectives constitute blatant stereotype description, the family and educational institutions
reinforce these assumed sex-related traits. The speaker perceives
herself in these terms and fulfills these prophecies. Her continued promise to "be good" (p. 120), to be "sweet" (p. 121), fulfills her role as the inessential "Other"[69] and functions more
profoundly as her apology for being a woman, and a sullied
woman at that. In some ways, she has already been conditioned
by society to accept the penalties of her sexuality. She cunningly
observes: "They don't like you to tell them you're unhappy because of them. If you do, they think you're possessive and exacting. And then they hate you" (p. 122). Writing about stunted
relationships did little to prevent Parker from living them.
Parker experienced much of this feeling of repression and psychic rage in her affair with Garrett, yet continued this punishing pattern in her life, despite recognizing it in her work.

Filled with self-loathing and a sense of betrayal, the
speaker has been used by her lover and is the victim of a double
standard of sexuality, one that Parker implicitly intends the

reader to comprehend. The narrator observes: "he's so sure of me, so sure," and then, characteristically, switches to the plural "they" in the following reflection: "I wonder why *they* hate you as soon as *they* are sure of you" (emphasis added; p. 123). As for her own view of this matter, she concludes: "*I* should think it would be so sweet to be sure" (emphasis added; p. 123).

But her view as a woman is trivialized, and her sense of abuse and even shame is intensified. In addition to the taboos and inhibitions cultivated by her education and by society are the feelings of disgust that emanate from the erotic experience itself.[70] Hence, the speaker's sense of suffering, which she confides to God as "bad, bad suffering," carries a potent dose of self-hate, masochism, and unconscious guilt.[71] Her purity lost to herself, her power over her lover dissipated through consummation, her pride depleted by her social trespass, the speaker's contradictory behavior forms a cumulative picture of private anguish weighted with self-recrimination and strangely mixed with flights of pure human rage. It is no wonder she rails at God, "You're so safe . . . Nothing can touch You; no one can twist Your heart in his hands" (p. 120). Denied the option for sexual fulfillment and erotic pleasure, the speaker's sense of self and her lovemaking as a woman revolve instead around the feeling of general loss. For a woman, physical love often implies a sense of loss, as in the loss of virginity, the loss of reputation, the loss of purity, while for a man, sexual experience is more frequently defined as a gain, a coming of manhood, a sexual triumph, a conquest. The amount of damage inflicted on women by the assumption that their sexuality constitutes impurity is probably inestimable.

In this sense, the speaker now regards her abandonment by her lover as a judgment. Her sense of alienation, sustained by the tormenting silence of the phone, is complete. It follows that whatever guilt she now experiences originates in some personal action that she feels has been a violation of society's code of morality. The emerging view of women revolves around the notion that, as a woman, the protagonist is forced to walk the delicate line between the expectations of her social role and the desires of her inner self. A deadly battle rages beneath the lighthearted surface.

Although the expected telephone call is only two hours and ten minutes late (it is ten minutes past seven as the story opens, and he promised to call at five), the narrator's buried rage surfaces with a vengeance. Why does she react so violently to this delay? What deeper significance does the phone call carry with it that makes every moment's wait so unendurable?

The telephone call will carry with it the assurance that what the narrator did was somehow "not bad." "If he doesn't phone me, I'll know God is angry with me. . . That will be a sign" (p. 121). But the speaker has already sentenced herself and her actions: "It was bad. I knew it was bad. All right, God, send me to hell. You think You're frightening me with Your Hell, don't You? You think Your Hell is worse than mine?" (p. 121). The psychological and spiritual condemnation that names her suffering as a hell bestows almost archetypal qualities upon legions of anonymous women who have experienced similar emotions.

As the symbolic instrument of the speaker's rejuvenation, the phone itself is invested with special meaning. A substitute for the man for whom she feels repressed rage, the telephone is attacked as a "damned, ugly, shiny thing" (p. 120). She threatens to pull out its "filthy roots" and smash its "smug black face in little bits" (p. 120), unless it rings at once. Certainly the need to hurt and destroy some tangible and solid substance satisfies her displaced anger. Her depiction of the phone endowed with human attributes as a "damned, ugly, shiny thing" suggest associations to her lover with good reasons, as does her desire to "pull out its filthy roots" and smash its smug face "in little bits." It comes as no surprise that later, in a clash of contradictory emotions, the speaker screams, "I wish I could hurt him like hell" (p. 121), followed by "that's a terrible wish. That's a lovely wish" (p. 122).

In the grip of this hopelessness, the speaker switches to self-pity and paranoia. Having conceded that men, in general "hate you whenever you say anything you really think," she adds perceptively, "You always have to keep playing little games" (p. 122). This feminine deception depicted by Parker underscores the ongoing disparity between the sexes and dramatizes the gulf between masculine and feminine perspective.

The humor derived from the narrator's seemingly comic and disproportionate reactions to the mute telephone cannot detract from the fundamental tragedy over which the speaker presides. The sense of her purgatory should not be taken lightly. The irrational flights of panic, the nearly crazed emotional outbursts, the deep sense of loneliness, guilt, and anguish followed by sadistic and destructive invectives recount in the first person the experiences of female suffering. In spite of all her efforts, the woman cannot rid herself of negative male definitions that she herself imposes. She has sentenced herself to an infected world of self-loathing, a "hell" that is worse than God's. Her prayer to the blessed Father in Heaven, to "let him call," which in a metaphoric sense, gives her absolution and redemption, remains unanswered, and the childlike counting at the end is no less pathetic than the suffering pleas at the beginning.

Although masked by humor and characterized by exaggeration, foolish behavior and incongruities, at its heart, "A Telephone Call" is actually a story of sexual distrust[72] and betrayal, as told from a woman's narrative perspective. Since the woman of the story is not portrayed as an equal to her male lover, and since the male voice is unheard, indeed unknown, the hidden emphasis in the piece revolves around the consequences of outward male rejection and subtle male subjugation as perceived by the narrator. The extension of that subjugation is evidenced in the symbolic count at the end of the story. Suspecting that their relationship is over now that they have had sex, she rationalizes, "Five, ten fifteen, twenty, twenty-five, thirty, thirty-five. . ." (p. 124). The empty ritual of denied action maintains metaphorically the passivity of the speaker. As an objective correlative for feminine passivity, the protagonist bides her time and fills empty space, hoping to derive her identity and definition by being acted upon, rather than by acting out her will.

Despite the promises to action, the speaker remains inert. The pendulum of emotion, manifested in the speaker's constant ambivalence, compose the structural base, as well as the thematic tension of this story. The speaker's identity, which divides itself in dichotomous personalities, exists as a response to the silence of the phone, which stands mute, the object of her impotent rage. Parker's presentation of the solitary, overwrought protagonist, whose aberrant behavior fluctuates between self-hate and self-deception, is more than a portrait of inappropriate and childish female hysteria. Her anxiety is an adult's trauma, which she speaks of movingly in her last sequence.

In the final lines of the monologue, the speaker talks of pride. She begs God to keep her from phoning—in her mind, the final humiliation: "Let me still have just a little bit of pride." But she adds, rather cryptically: "The real pride, the big pride, is in having no pride" (p. 123). Is this a veiled message from the promptings of her true nature admonishing her to disengage herself finally from the false "pride" of her sex, i.e., the fake mantle of womanhood that extracts fraudulent behavior in the name of propriety and lack of authenticity in the name of accommodation? Perhaps, this moment brings us closer to the authorial values of Parker than any other in the short monologue. However, Parker is quick to make herself immune from this connection by deflating the possibility with the lines: "This is such a little thing, for me to be bringing in pride, for me to be making such a fuss about" (p. 123).

With a sense of exhaustion, the speaker utters the real truth hovering at the center of the story. She calls the people who write books about sweet and true romantic love liars. "Don't they know it's a lie . . . God damned lie . . . What do they have to tell about that for, when they know how it hurts. Damn them, damn them, damn them" (p. 124).

Even a hasty perusal of "A Telephone Call" will underscore the fact that Parker is not guilty of perpetuating the lie of romantic love. The reader who probes deeply discovers beneath the surface humor, the contemptuous despair of a woman who finally defines herself and her relationship with her man in terms of disappointment, rejection, guilt, and humiliation. Behind the parody of social behavior, there is a sentient being suffering slowly and alone for her "sins" as a woman.

Parker captured the essence of this female wretchedness, for both herself and her narrator in a poem entitled, "Two Volume Novel," interestingly included in her second verse publication, *Sunset Gun* (1928), which she dedicated to John Garrett:

> The sun's gone dim, and
> The moon's turned black;
> For I loved him, and
> He didn't love back.

Oddly, Parker, who exhibited fierce personal autonomy and independence in so much of her life as a writer, was unable to extricate herself from emotional dependence on men like Garrett, whose rejection and intolerable behavior were a source of heartache and misery for her. She accepted abuse, dominance, and infidelity with regularity. Garrett disappeared from her life abruptly, and she seldom spoke of him.

However, in 1931, her affair with John McClain was similarly painful and ultimately sordid. Dorothy repeated her penchant for heartbreak. McClain, a recent college football star, and young reporter for the *New York Sun*, met Dorothy and saw her as easy passage to a more celebrated literary life. Athletic, well built, handsome, a blatant social climber, McClain, encouraged by an assortment of women who ecstatically assured him of his unusual sexual abilities, took up with Dorothy despite their differences in age. He was twenty-seven; she was thirty-eight. According to Keats, "Mr. McClain, to use his own words, considered himself to be a hell of a swordsman, a he-whore," and he bragged to friends that he intended to "roll up a score" with well-known women in society, on the stage, and in the literary world."[73]

Like the pathetic creature of her own fiction, Dorothy, despite advice to the contrary, fell passionately in love with him. She idealized their romance and threw herself at McClain, often telephoning him daily and waiting anxiously for his responses. She checked with his friends, took abuse from him for having a "voracious sexual appetite," and time and again endured his infidelities. Within a short time, McClain felt smothered. There were violent quarrels and sometimes public spectacles. He began to complain that Parker would not leave him alone. She called incessantly, wanting to know his whereabouts, why he had not kept their engagements, why he would not see her.

There were a series of terrible midnight calls to McClain with threats of suicide and hysterical outbursts. Even when she knew he had moved on to other women, she strangely allowed herself to be dominated. "His body went to his head," she quipped, but inwardly she anguished and continued to accept his insults.

Parker ultimately appeared in the ridiculous role of the fading older woman, hopelessly pursuing the virile young man, tragically grateful for any moments he condescended to allot to her. When it was clear that McClain was through with her, she moved out of the Algonquin without a word to her friends. She did apparently leave a message with the bell captain, short and to the point, "I've gone away."[74]

Though her affair with McClain took place three years after the publication of "A Telephone Call," it revisited with dismal and ironic accuracy the same emotional landscape in fact, that Parker had so meticulously plotted in fiction.

The Fallen Angel:
"Big Blonde" (1929)

"Big Blonde"[75] was Dorothy Parker's most intensely autobiographical piece of fiction. The story, a virtual confessional, was a rendering of loneliness, depression, suicide attempts, alcoholism and ill-fated loves; it was a kaleidoscope of Parker's life. It was also Parker's most concentrated effort to prove herself as a writer of substantive fiction, and possibly the finest story she ever wrote. It won the O. Henry Award for best story of 1929.

Set in New York, in the 1920s, "Big Blonde" chronicles the alcoholic downfall of Hazel Morse. A "large fair woman, of the type that incites some men when they use the word, 'blonde' to click their tongues and wag their heads roguishly," Hazel was sensual, fun-loving and popular, the model of what men call a "good sport" (p. 187). Her view of life was simple:

> Popularity seemed to her to be worth all the work that had to be put into its achievement. Men like you because you were fun, and when they liked you they took you out, and there you were. (p. 187)

In her mid-thirties as the story opens, Hazel regards her past as an "imperfect film, dealing with the actions of strangers" (p. 187). Through a series of flashbacks, the reader is taken back to images of Hazel's life as a young woman in her twenties employed as a "model in a wholesale dress establishment"

(p. 187) and is ultimately brought up to her meeting with Herbie.

We recall that Henry Rothschild's garment business was a world that Dorothy knew and reviled. Parker's memories of the Seventh Avenue trade, and all that was associated with it, contributed to her hatred of a past that humiliated and embarrassed her. It is from this coarse environment that Hazel seeks escape.

After years of playing the good sport, the glamour of dating dimmed, and Hazel now nearing thirty and fearful about her job, marries Herbie Morse, to gain stability and retire into what she expects will be a conventional marriage. However, without the facade of the jolly, cheerful, good-time girl, she became a bore to Herbie, who resorts more and more to drinking in order to restore some vitality to their relationship. Although Hazel herself "hated the taste of liquor" (p. 193), she is nevertheless pressed into a drinking partnership by Herbie, who encourages her to "get boiled" (p. 192) so they can have some fun. Soon a regular companion to his indulgences, Hazel's drinking increases. She began drinking alone; it got her through the 'blues,' just little, short drinks all through the day. "It was only with Herbie that alcohol made her nervous and quick in offense" (p. 193)

The increasing quarrels with Herbie combined with her growing dependence on alcohol, drives Herbie into abusive behavior, and finally away altogether. Drinking heavily and left to her own devices, Hazel resorts to the one familiar core of her life and learns to trade sex for the illusion of security.

Discarded by a succession of increasingly inferior men, as age and alcohol extract their price, Hazel is finally rejected by her latest lover, Art, a "short and fat and exacting" (p. 202) man who is disgusted by her lack of gaiety. Driven by the deep despair and loneliness of her life and no longer capable of being assuaged by alcohol, Hazel finally faces her latent desire for suicide. She secures enough veronal to kill herself, and after an overdose, dozes off, grimly repeating the phrase "Gee, I'm nearly dead" (p. 205). Ironically, she is saved from death to return in the last scene to a life that she prays will let her "be able to get drunk, please, please," she begs desperately, always "drunk" (p. 205).

The story apparently formed in Parker's mind during a three-week stay at Presbyterian Hospital, where she was recovering from an emergency operation for acute appendicitis. It was a low period in her life. Her affair with John Garrett was over. According to friends she was "half soused" and murderously insulting a good deal of the time; she seldom had money, and she was seriously beginning to question her ability as a writer. As she pondered her own failures, depressed by the absence of a completed novel, and struck by the vicissitudes of her life, she called forth from her depths the heroine of the story, Hazel Morse, casting a pitiless eye on the fictional counterpart of herself.

Written with detached objectivity, Parker turned away from emotionalism, carefully selecting facts from the chaos of a reality which she herself knew well. Parker captured with cold, clear precision; the experiences of a woman's life set against the meretriciousness and empty values of New York society in the 1920's.

Though Parker did not set out with a feminist agenda, and few critics have authentically acknowledged that there is one, Parker's close examination of the female consciousness of Hazel Morse awakens the reader to the ways in which women are victims both of society and of individual men.

The aesthetic effect of the story draws its strength from the haunted atmosphere of pain, of despair, of vague inarticulated sufferings, of doubt and unfulfillment, of the dark haze of unconscious longings that hints at an inner life buried and hidden in the deep channels of Hazel's soul.

The central issue of "Big Blonde" concerns Hazel Morse's continuing struggle to define herself and achieve security and acceptance by the American male. Aware that the "good sport" (p. 187) image will ingratiate her with men, Hazel plays this role, even though it is unnatural and finally anathema to her. From the opening descriptive passages, Parker makes it clear that Hazel Morse devotes herself to being popular with men. "No other form of diversion, simple or more complicated, drew her attention" (p. 187).

Our first insight into the scaffolding of Hazel Morse's true identity derives not from the initial physical description of her "as a large fair woman that incites some men when they use the word 'blonde' to click their tongues," but rather from the subsequent small details that she "prided herself upon her small feet and suffered for her vanity, boxing them in snub-toed high heeled slippers of the shortest bearable size" (p. 187). This particular literal detail regarding the ill-fitting slippers, may be linked to Hazel's designation as a woman who has the function to fulfill society's conception of a woman's role, no matter how painful that conception may be.

Parker's immediate attention in the second sentence of the story to the "snub-toed high heeled slippers," a material emblem of a specific time and place, also serves to set the ironic tone of absurd tragedy and painful humor in the piece. Just as she jams her small feet into her smaller unsuitable slippers in order to achieve some ridiculous sense of fashionable appearance, Hazel forces herself into a series of uncomfortable stereotypical roles that society similarly demands. Both accommodations ultimately prove to be painful.

Despite the fact that the story is Parker's longest and most panoramic in its use of time, contrary to her usual limited concentration on one scene, the extended focus on Hazel Morse over a prolonged period carries an intensity of its own. In its depiction of the birth and growth of alcoholism, suicidal despair and the brutality of a dissolute life, the story is astonishingly realistic.

The evenings spent laughing at men's jokes and telling men that she "loved their neckties," achieved for Hazel over the years the specious benefits of barroom popularity. "Men liked her, and she took it for granted that the liking of many men was a desirable thing" (p. 187).

Parker points out that Hazel herself "never pondered if she might not be better occupied doing something else." She was "fun," and she was a "good sport," and "men liked a good sport," and that seemed quite enough for Hazel (p. 187).

Hazel is drawn to Herb, whose frisky personality and speakeasy habits reflect Hazel as we first know her, "a good sport" and a party regular. The fact that he drank "largely," Hazel found "entertaining" (p. 188). She liked Herbie immediately, and sensing that her image as a good sport had become more "conscientious than spontaneous" (p. 189), Hazel delighted in Herbie's proposal.

They were married six weeks after they met and Hazel was thrilled in her new life. For the first time in years, she felt as through she could relax and stop worrying about being a social misfit. However, as quickly as she drops the "good sport" role, she adopts another stereotypical role as the tender and submissive wife. In the first months of her marriage she threw herself passionately into domesticity, cooking, cleaning, attending to the details of her little flat. She missed none of the old crowd and was content to spend evenings peacefully at home with Herbie. Wedded and relaxed, her marriage was a delightful new game, a comforting peace. There was, however, one problem. "Herbie was not amused" (p. 189).

This change in his wife, the voluntary isolation that Hazel found novel and sweet, palled with a fierce suddenness. "It was as if one night, sitting with her in the steam-heated living-room, he would ask no more; and the next thing he was through and done with the whole thing" (p. 190).

The subsequent failure of her marriage is linked to the fact that Hazel cannot understand what Herbie wants, and cannot revert to what she was. "She was completely bewildered by what happened to their marriage" (p. 190). They seemed to move from lovers to enemies without any transition. A powerful domesticity had taken hold of Hazel. "She wanted what she called a nice Home" (p. 190). Herbie restlessly sought something else, finding an outlet for his boredom with her and his marriage in whiskey and carousing. The marriage was doomed. "She could not manage him"[76] (p. 190).

Though Parker does not make it explicit, it seems clear that Hazel's perception of marriage is based on the popular bogus myths of the day, rooted in stereotypes of blissful domesticity. The portrait of Hazel both as a good sport and as a good wife reinforce the one-dimensionality of her female role as a response to traditional social myths. Hazel has no clear concept of herself as an individual woman. Her essence as she is presented is primarily derived in terms of her relationship to men. For all practical purposes, her aspirations in the story revolve around being either a good sport or a good wife.

The signs of Hazel's inability to control the direction of her life lead us to suspect that she is deficient in maturity and judgment. Her romantic conception of herself in the marriage is just as faulty as the good sport persona of the speakeasies. Neither is a sharply focused, fully realized vision of life. Indeed, as her name, Hazel, suggests, she lives in a perpetual haze, discerning everything through blurred perceptions, from the misty melancholies of her early life to the darkly unfocused distortion of her alcoholic benders. Her inability to "see" clearly, either drunk or sober, is a major recurring motif in the story, manifested and sometimes concealed in the metaphoric patterning of the work.

For example, Parker tells us in the second paragraph of the story, "She [Hazel] was not a woman given to recollections" (p. 187). Although only in her mid-thirties, Hazel's past is described as a "blurred and flickering" series of events like an "imperfect film, dealing with the actions of strangers" (p. 187). The single memory she has of her family is described as a vague remembrance of a "hazy widowed mother," whose passing is rather hauntingly referred to as a "deferred death" (p. 1987).

Limited by a lack of intellectual acuity, Hazel's instinctive life is foremost. Openly vulnerable, simple and unselectively emotional, she adapts to her domestic life with the same lack of retrospection and modulation that characterized her life as a party girl. As she laughed easily in the speakeasy, she cries easily at home.

> To her who had laughed so much, crying was delicious. All sorrow became her sorrow; she was tenderness. She would cry long and softly over newspaper accounts of kidnapped babies, deserted wives, unemployed men, strayed cats, heroic dogs. (p. 189)

Her lavish weeping and inordinate melancholy over the abandoned, the deserted, and the strayed, harbingers of Hazel's own future, serve only to annoy and alienate Herb.

Herb's solution to his domestic boredom is to press Hazel into drinking. Her conversion to alcoholism is swift, and Herb's fury matched her despair. It was during those days that Hazel "began the hatred of being alone that she was never to overcome" (p. 193).

When Herb leaves, Mrs. Martin, the great blonde woman of forty next door, a promise of Hazel's future, provides easy entry into the world of liquor and lovers that became Hazel's permanent way of life. Bouncing between the antipodes of drunkenness and sex, Hazel has only one image to live up to, the "good sport" image, the only model left to her that she knows with any certainty.

As Parker later revealed, her husband Eddie similarly urged her to drink with him; in fact to explore effective, "proper," drinking until she discovered, under his tutelage, that Scotch whiskey, without water, though expensive, was quick and dependable. She did not realize at this time the extent of Eddie's addictions, nor that Eddie's alcoholism required a drinking partner. Clearly, at the beginning, Parker did not understand that she was dealing with a sick man. Originally, she tried to modify his drinking, urging him to stop, cajoling him, scolding him and ultimately covering up for him. She often called in to his office to report him ill, creating absurd excuses for his absences. She devoted herself to him during these times, putting him to bed, comforting his hangovers, assuaging his drunken and often abusive personality, following the common pattern of those enablers who live with and often ultimately themselves become alcoholics.

To lessen Eddie's endless reproaches about his drinking, Parker finally, apprehensively, joined him, later claiming that drinking together meant an hour or two of carousing revelry, cock-eyed behavior and wild outrageous times that broke up the arguing and scolding. Eventually, sobered or too "boozed-up" to care, she would turn belligerent and contemptuous. The inevitable scene ensued. Eddie would rage at her, calling her a "rotten sport", a nag, and "a crab," phrases that found their way verbatim into the reenactments between Hazel and Herb.

Despite Eddie's dependence and growing reliance on both drugs and alcohol, Parker, whose reputation in public was allegedly callous, hardened, and notoriously ruthless, nevertheless in private she was surprisingly devoted to Eddie. For reasons few people ever understood, she held on with him in what appears to have been her insistence to persevere in a relationship that was mutually destructive and unsatisfying. Often he stayed out all night, refusing to say where he had been. Occasionally, she would wake up with bruises, and at least once with a black eye. To tranquilize herself, she discovered that little nips of liquor throughout the day could keep her mellow and hazy, a condition that made work, to an already undisciplined writer, virtually impossible.

She also discovered that drinking with Eddie made her nervous—while drinking without him made her cheerful and clever. The best drinking, she concluded, was with Benchley and the Round Tablers. Fueled with liquor, fired by masculine camaraderie, the Round Tablers readily encouraged Parker's sardonic comments and flippant humor. Eddie did not. But here, amongst the snobbery and cherished exclusivity of the group, Parker was loved and appreciated; Eddie was from the beginning an awkward outsider, and ultimately the target of Parker's cruel invectives. In the end, Eddie, like Herb, left. Ironically, Eddie died at the age of thirty-nine from what appeared to be an overdose of sleeping powders, which may have been accidental.

Though it is alleged that Dorothy never appeared to be entirely drunk, it is also true that she was probably seldom sober. It was this "hazy" quality, pendulating between extremes of drunken sanctums, and fuzzy realities that Parker captured with such poignancy in Hazel Morse.

Though one hesitates to dismiss too simply the complex factors that contributed to Hazel's drinking during this period,[77] Parker indicated that Hazel drank in order to keep herself dazed and woozy. "She lived in the haze of it" (p.193), a reiteration of the thematic element of Hazel's own obscurity as well as Hazel's obscure vision.

The many references to the word "haze" (the word and its variants are used at least six times) as a reverberation of Hazel's personality, indicate a great deal about Hazel as a specific female type, apart from her relationship with men. Even prior to her marriage to Herb and before her drinking days, she is described as simple and unreflective. She has few original thoughts, and accepts the ideas of "the other substantially built blondes in whom she found her friends" (p. 187). Later she seeks the sedation of alcohol and the perpetual haze of a life that is neither "noticeably drunk and seldom sober" (p. 197), doubtless as a result of her individual chemistry. It may be argued then, that Hazel's drinking problem, which forms the core of the story, is self-generated, not necessarily the result of a male-female conflict. Perhaps her drinking and her demise are predicable conclusions to a muddled and vulnerable personality incapable of facing life directly.

This argument notwithstanding, we must also concede that despite years of working as a model, frequenting speakeasies and playing the good sport, Hazel was not a drinker. It was

Herb who pressed her into drinking, who was "glad to see her drink" although she "hated the taste of liquor" (p. 192), and his abuse and desertion exacerbated her loneliness and need for alcohol.

Her drinking "blurred sharp things for her. She lived in the haze of it. Her life had taken on a dream-like quality. Nothing was astonishing" (p. 193). As to her succession of lovers, "in her haze, she never recalled how men entered her life and left it. There were no surprises" (p. 200). Time coalesced into an indistinguishable blur. "She never knew dates, nor was sure of the day of the week," and even the thought of death lent her "a drowsy cheer" (p. 201). The recurring pert slogan "Here's mud in your eye" (p. 205), threaded through the piece with regularity, ironically underscores Hazel's limited and indistinct view of life around her. Yet, Hazel, for all her limitations, or perhaps because of them, has a decided poignancy about her. Much of this poignancy is achieved by the manner in which Parker links the workings of Hazel's inner life with the opaque apprehension of her outer reality.

Part of the deficiency of Hazel's emotional substructure is Hazel's inability to place issues clearly in her life, the metaphoric equivalent of her own muddled identity. Consider the following passages related to the recollection of significant events in Hazel's mind:

I. *The onset of alcoholism*
She could not recall the definite day that she started drinking herself. There was nothing separate about her days. Like drops upon a windowpane, they ran together and trickled away. She had been married six months; then a year; then three years. (p. 191).

II. *Her first extra-marital affair*
Again, she could not find a definite day to fix the beginning of Ed's proprietorship. It became his custom to kiss her on the mouth when he came in, as well for farewell, and he gave her little quick kisses of approval all through the evening. She liked this rather more than she disliked it. She never thought of his kisses when she was not with him. (p. 194)

III. *Suicide*
There was no settled, shocked moment when she first thought of killing herself; it seemed to her as if the idea had always been with her. She pounced upon all the accounts of suicides in the newspa-

pers. There was an epidemic of self-killings or maybe it was just that she searched for the stories of them so eagerly that she found many. To read of them aroused reassurance in her; she felt a cozy solidarity with the big company of the voluntary dead. (p. 201)

In these passages, Hazel is unable to identify with exactness what is happening to her—and more importantly, is unable to assimilate its significance. On the surface she appears dull, insentient. Her life and its events seem indistinct to her. This lack of introspective ability gives her a certain kind of vulnerability and potential for abuse. Is she merely vacuous and unfeeling? An unimaginative dumb clod? Upon closer scrutiny, these passages of vague associations have a distinct emotional quality that Parker subtlety links to the heightened moments of Hazel's life. Hence, what Hazel feels is more remarkable than what she thinks or what she claims to remember. Devoid of outward verbal fluency, her inner emotional life, is nevertheless alive and lucid with feelings that are palpable to her. Hazel seems unable to recall specific factual details of time and place, but by contrast she expresses poignantly the emotions associated with these events. In this way, Parker draws sympathy for Hazel.

In passage I, for example, she cannot recall the definite day that she started drinking, since there was nothing "separate about her days," yet she thinks of these indistinct days as "drops upon a window-pane" that "ran together and trickled away" (p. 191).

In passage II, the day that Ed's courtship began is unknown to her, yet she is aware that she "liked his kisses," when she was with him and "that she never thought of his kisses when she was not with him" (p. 194).

In passage III, though she does not recall when suicide entered her mind, she feels a "cozy solidarity" with the "voluntary dead" (p. 201).

In each reflection, Hazel's thoughts are a mixture of vague, blocked memories and sharp, recollected sentiment—sentiment that is virtually poetic in its resonance, and sympathetic in its appeal.

Thus far Hazel has been cast into two different roles, both of which fail to give her personal happiness. The indulgent image of compulsive domesticity proves just as disastrous as the artificial personality of the speakeasies. Prosaic, simple, neither bright nor ambitious, Hazel sought merely to conform to a certain narrow image. Male-dependent and limited in her sensibilities, she had no further wish than to fit into a prescribed role, rather than to create one.

What was the prescribed role of the alleged "emancipated" woman of the twenties that Hazel presumably epitomized? Why did it fail to produce fulfillment? Is Hazel an example of something fraudulent in our national life? The era was characterized as fast and flippant, a social show of people on the town, a "revolution in manner and morals."[78] However, as in Hazel's case, behind the flippancy was often a buried sensitivity and a private loneliness.

It was during prohibition that women began to drink publicly, and like her "emancipated" lady-friends of the time, idle, untrained, with nothing on their minds but to make a man happy, Hazel had to drink and to keep drinking to show what good fellows they were and what boozy fun they could have. In the speakeasy environment of the wise crack, Hazel incarnates the persistent sardonic theme of the vulnerability of certain woman. The women at Jimmy's, Hazel's hangout, are the unhappy victims of their own sexuality and the false "emancipation" of the period. Yoked to a merry image of fake gaiety, Hazel is actually unable to express herself or her unhappiness throughout the story. She is not permitted the right to admit her miseries, her fatigue, her longings.

Before her marriage, Hazel learned to play out a "couple of thousand evenings of being a good sport among her male acquaintances" (p. 188). During her marriage she hid her feelings, fearing Herb's accusations that she was "crabbing" (p. 190). After her marriage collapsed, she was warned by her barroom boyfriends, "Nobody wants to hear other people's troubles, sweetie. What you got to do, you got to be a sport and forget it. See? Well, slip us a little smile, then. That's my girl" (p. 199). The superficial muddled personality is in some ways the result of never being allowed or at least encouraged to express her private emotions.

Her forced gaiety and her crude beauty are her only ticket to survival. She holds on to the notion that "men liked her" even though, paradoxically, it is this very idea that inhibits and destroys her. In reality, Hazel continually capitulates to male values, which she herself adopts as the standard. She vainly struggles to be what men want her to be and evolves no other values of her own. Her marriage, rather than a discovery, was a surrender to Herbie's needs, and because she could not "manage" him, the marriage deteriorated. Herbie's desertion leaves her with no resources but to return to the speakeasy, where again she is defined against a background of sexual relationships.

In her description of the women at Jimmy's Parker paints a picture of the messy, pathetic, befuddled speakeasy women who pretend merriment and hide their loneliness in the nightly ritual of recycled make believe for the benefit of male companionship.

> The woman at Jimmy's looked remarkably alike, and this was curious, for, through feuds, removals, and opportunities of more profitable contacts, the personnel of the group changed constantly. Yet always the newcomers resembled those whom they replaced. They were all big women and stout, broad of shoulder and abundantly breasted with faces thickly clothed in soft, high colored flesh. They laughed loud and often, showing opaque and lusterless teeth like squares of crockery. There was about them the health of the big, yet a slightly unwholesome suggestion of stubborn preservation. They might have been thirty-six or forty-five or anywhere between. (p. 198)

In this assemblage of atrophied females, Hazel ultimately takes her place, as Charley, Ed, Sidney, Bill, Fred and the legions of admirers pass in and out of her dazed existence. Stoic, even-tempered, good natured, and generous, Hazel confronts her life, making the best of things, holding on, and above all, clinging to the image of herself as a "good sport." Hazel actually learned to be a good sport about everything. She was a good sport about going to bed with men, and in return they gave her money and presents. She was a good sport about not complaining, not crabbing, and not nagging. Being a good sport was a lesson she had learned well.

Even in the early days of Herb's abuse, when he flew into rages, stayed out all night, blackened her eye, and blunted her emotions until her heart felt sore, and her "mind turned like an electric fan" (p. 194), Hazel learned that the unforgivable thing for a woman was to be a "rotten sport" (p. 194). "Crab, crab, crab, crab, crab" (p. 191), Herbie would scream at her until she usually apologized in bed and promised to change and make "everything swell" (p. 192), though she never had the slightest idea what she had done wrong. Thus Hazel learned that marriage was a private ordeal in which the wife had a special duty as a woman to create gaiety and serve male needs even at the price of self-destruction. Yet Hazel, like many of her sex, oddly welcomed the role that society had ordained for them as willing destroyers of themselves.[79]

Like many of Parker's fictional women, Hazel's conscious language disguises the terrors, doubts, and fears of a private life which carries a good deal of masochism and self-contempt. We see that her conscious language is rife with the banalities of her social caste devoid of verbal richness. Only by endowing familiar slogans, colloquialism with broad irony, does her consiousness find a potent form of self-expression.[80] Thus, her snappy slogans, "I'm swell" and "Mud in your eye" serve to reinforce her role as a good sport. But since this is her only conscious language, she cannot forsake it, even in crisis. The suicide scene provides an example.

Played out by the sordidness of her life, rejected by her current lover, and no longer able to dull the pain of her existence with liquor, Hazel chooses to finalize her death by suicide. The deserted streets, the wretchedness in her body, the sight of a screaming horse, the disappointments in her pointless evening, combine to motivate Hazel to uncork the vials of veronal she had stored carefully and swallow enough tablets to kill herself. As she looks in the mirror and yawns, Hazel remarks, "Guess I'll go to bed . . . Gee I'm nearly dead" (p. 205). The colloquialism, with its double-edged irony, amuses her enough so that she comments, "That's a hot one" (p. 205), and she drifts off to sleep, and to what she believes is an end to her miseries.

Yet, the irony continues to operate in a number of less obvious ways. On the narrative level, the brevity, the levity, and the quality of the remarks "Gee I'm nearly dead . . . That's a hot one," juxtaposed against the grimness of the situation, produce clear ironic contrast. However, in addition, the statement also functions as a bitter commentary on Hazel's own condition as essentially both lifeless and worn out. Furthermore, her failure actually to die violates our expectations, creates an ironic relationship between Hazel and her fate, and intensifies both the dark humor and the pitiful pathos in both statement and situation. Neither her words nor her actions have the meaning or results she planned or predicted. Her suicide fails. She is sentenced to life.

The fictionalized event was a virtual duplication from a dark period in Parker's life. In 1926, Parker had discovered veronal, taking it when Scotch no longer succeeded in putting her out. She was able to secure the barbituate by making special trips to Newark, New Jersey, where the drug was available without prescription. She accumulated a stock of pills and kept their use a secret from Dr. Barach, who was at this time treating her for depression.

Particularly miserable over the loss of the airedale dog that Eddie had given her, physically ravaged by her drinking, which according to Dr. Barach had reached "pathological proportions," Dorothy returned drunk one night to her hotel, and like Hazel, sought the cache of veronal she had stored in her dressing table. Parker swallowed the tablets, then laid herself on the bed and waited.

According to Dr. Barach, she saved herself by throwing a glass through the window at the last moment. Parker herself suggests that her attempt failed because she had not taken enough pills and more importantly because the maid Ivy (named Nettie in the story) discovers her at the last moment and calls for help.

When she awakened in the hospital two days later, Parker was outraged at Dr. Barach for having saved her, echoing the same disappointment that Hazel utters. After the nurses told Parker she was lucky to be alive, she cried bitterly at her bad luck in failing to die, and pretentiously and pathetically, striving to be witty, begged for a drink. Barach kept her in the hospital to dry her out, but did not realize that Parker was receiving a steady supply of liquor from Heywood Broun, also a patient of Barach's, who provided alcohol from a hip flask he brought on his daily visits to her in the hospital. Barach was later to say of the group that they were all living desperate, false, unstable lives. They forced themselves to be witty, rejecting seriousness as unfashionable, succumbing to self-imposed constant pressure to be clever. They needed each other because they knew something was missing, and they needed the security the group gave them. One result of their insecurity was their intolerable self-absorption and arrogance. "Nearly all of them had a terrible malicious streak."[81] Though Parker's attempt at her life was hushed up, and predictably treated as a comic bungle by insiders, the trauma of it was recorded vividly in "Big Blonde."

According to one recent feminist study, suicide has particular significance to women. The largest single category of both attempted and completed suicides are found amongst women, usually housewives. Women "attempt" to kill themselves more than men.[82]

Erwin Stengel and Nancy Cook's study on suicide finds that "suicidal acts by men resulted in death more frequently than those by women. Two-thirds of all suicidal acts committed by men, but only one-third of those committed by women ended fatally."[83] It is probably true that while "men commit actions; women commit gestures."[84] However, female suicide is not so much a call for help as it is an act of resignation and helplessness. According to Phyllis Chesler, "suicide attempts are the grand rites of 'femininity,' i.e., ideally, women are supposed to 'lose' in order 'to win'."[85] Accordingly, it is of more than passing interest that as Hazel faces the mirror after she has downed the lethal dose of tablets, she loudly mimics Art's last warning to her: "For God's sake, try and cheer up by Thursday, will you," to which she bitterly responds, "Well, you know what he can do. He and the whole lot of them" (p. 205). Hazel's aborted suicide may perhaps be seen as a masochistic form of self-criticism and self-hatred inherent in her nature as a woman, but it may also be seen as a final attempt to reject the female role she has come to despise by paying for it with her life.[86]

Ironically Hazel is saved by a callous male physician whose drinking and love play with a cheap floozy are interrupted by Hazel's emergency. In effect, by restoring her body, Hazel's male saviour resurrects her for the continued patriarchal expropriation she had hoped to escape.

It is tempting to see Hazel's choice of self-extinction as symbolic. The use of drugs, an extension of the dazed and bewildered state of Hazel's life as a woman, is suggestive. Her blundering efforts to make one clear statement of rejection as a woman outraged against her abusers is almost predictable.

Lying drugged on the bed, Hazel is momentarily free of the bondage of alcohol and men that have claimed her life.

> Mrs. Morse lay upon her back, one flabby, white arm flung up, the wrist against her forehead. Her stiff hair hung untenderly along her face. The bed covers were pushed down, exposing a deep square of soft neck and a pink nightgown, its fabric work uneven by many launderings; her great breasts, freed from their tight confines, sagged beneath her armpits. Now and then she made knotted snoring sounds, and from the corner of her opened mouth to the blurred turn of her jaw ran a line of crusted spittle. (p. 206)

The scene, reminiscent of her suicidal prototype Emma Bovary,[87] spares no detail of Hazel's utter demise.

When Hazel comes back to consciousness, Nettie, her colored maid, reminds her that the doctor said "he could have you arrested, doin' a thing like that. He was fit to be tied, here" (p. 209). Hazel responds miserably, "'Why couldn't he let me alone?' wails Mrs. Morse. 'Why the hell couldn't he have?'" (p. 209).

Hazel's "wail" is not only a protest, as Parker intends, against the perpetuation of a life already deemed miserable by its possessor, but it functions furthermore as the cry of a woman against the continued domination by and perhaps even dependence on men for life's meaning. Nevertheless, Hazel who has bungled her life, bungles her death as well.

The doctor who saves her, while muttering that she is a "nuisance" (p. 208), joins the parade of men in Hazel's life who never saw Hazel as anything but a compelling physical presence to which they might address themselves. The doctor's only comment about Hazel is "You couldn't kill her with an axe" (p. 208), a bitter ironic reverberation of Hazel's early statement about the Veronal, "Well, I guess I got enough to kill an ox" (p. 203).

Nowhere in the story is the depth of Hazel's desperation more harrowingly conveyed than through the image of the wretched horse that Hazel witnesses being beaten on the dismal night she decides to end her life.

> As she slowly crossed Sixth Avenue, consciously dragging one foot past the other, a big, scarred horse pulling a rickety ex-

press-wagon crashed to his knees before her. The driver swore and screamed and lashed the beast insanely, bringing the whip back over his shoulder for every blow, while the horse struggled to get a footing on the slippery asphalt. A group gathered and watched with interest. (p. 204)

This memorable scene incarnates Hazel's personal tragedy and the abuses of her life. In a feeling sense, the passage resonates with unprovoked brutality, unleashed against a helpless victim who is exhausted by the exploitation of a cruel master. In her dim way, Hazel comprehends this, and struggles to express the latent content of her vaguely aroused thoughts. "I saw a horse," she later says to Art, at Jimmy's. "Gee, I—a person feels sorry for horses. I—it isn't just horses. Everything's kind of terrible, isn't it?" (p. 204). The phonetic equation between Morse, Hazel's married name and "horse" evokes the abuses of her married life to Herbie while the metaphoric parallel between the mistreated animal and the mistreated Hazel in general seems clear. The tragic image of the horse reappears at the end of the story coupled with the painful champagne-colored slippers from the opening paragraph.

Cruelly rewarded with a life she doesn't want, Hazel wakes up in the hospital and is handed a card from her crude and erstwhile lover Art with the familiar admonition to "cheer up" (p. 209) by Thursday. The words effect an instant misery as though she were crushed between "great smooth stones" (p.209). In an epiphanic moment of unaccustomed clarity, a slow pageant of her life passes before her:

> Days spent lying in her flat, of evenings at Jimmy's being a good sport, making herself laugh and coo at Art and other Arts; she saw a parade of wary horses and shivering beggars, all beaten, driven, stumbling things. Her feet throbbed as if she had crammed them into the stubby champagne-colored slippers. (p. 209)

"The long parade of wary horses and shivering, beaten, driven, stumbling things" embody for Hazel a wretched and pathetic metaphor of her existence. Her capitulation to a society of good-time values and empty relationship passes through her emotional substrata with sharp clarity and lucidity that until now have remained unfocused.

That mental apprehension is translated unconsciously to her body, which supplies the physical confirmation of the failure and waste of her lifetime efforts to fit into a vulgar society. Her feet throbbed, "as if she had crammed them" into the symbolic champagne-colored slippers, and she felt her heart "swell and harden" (p. 209).

Parker has brought together in this passage all of the images of pain and suffering that Hazel had hoped to leave behind. In a lamentable gesture of defeat and resignation, Hazel and the maid Nettie share a drink. "You cheer up now," says Nettie. "Yeah," said Hazel. "Sure" (p. 210).

This final monosyllabic utterance, seasoned by the toughness of her experiences, summons all the bravery Hazel has and is capable of expressing. In classic understatement, Parker refuses to demand pity for Hazel, but precisely for this reason, Hazel earns it.

The story of Hazel Morse traces the steady downhill descent of a woman's wretched life. Jimmy's place existed in fact and Hazel existed somewhere in everyone's memory. Parker had described a female prototype of the twenties—not a whore—but a party girl, a fun lover and a pal to share bed and booze; a wise-cracker who could joke her way through the evening and show a guy a little fun. Yet in this view of women, Parker showed how little fun there was for a woman in that sort of "fun."

When Marion Capron asked Parker, "What about 'Big Blonde?' Where does the idea come from?" Parker responded, "I knew a lady—a friend of mine who went through holy hell. Just say I knew a woman once."[88]

Old Maids and Wives: "Horsie" (1932)

Dorothy Parker described 1932 as "this year of hell." Once again she attempted to kill herself with Veronal, after preparing a Will and Testament addressed to Benchley's attention. She directed any royalties on her books to the latest of her ill-fated lovers, John McClain, who had long since abandoned her for a wealthy Long Island socialite. McClain did not return as Dorothy wickedly predicted, "as soon as he had licked all the gilt off." Parker's consumption of sleeping powders on Thursday evening at the end of February was enough to make her ill, but not enough to claim her life. She called Dr. Barach, who shuttled her to the hospital, but did not diagnose her situation as life threatening. McClain cruelly announced that he considered her suicide attempt as a typical female trick to bring him back, a scheme that he claimed made him lose all respect for her. Parker recuperated with friends in the country, but soon returned to Manhattan and her nightly rounds of drinking and carousing.

By the end of winter, Parker was in serious financial trouble. She had long regarded the handling of money with disdain and often told friends she was "poorer than poverty itself." Broke and in debt, it became clear that she had to give diligent attention to completing her work and publishing her writings immediately. She selected for her subjects the targets she knew best—her friends—the rich socialites, the witty and elegant whose high priced company she pursued and exploited and subsequently derided and satirized.

Adele Lovett, lovely, blond, rich, and beautiful, who amused herself by cultivating the Round Table writers, became the object of Parker's ridicule in "Horsie,"[89] a story that criticizes the self-centeredness and callousness of the society that Parker inhabited and helped create. The story explores the contemporary myths of beauty. Parker, writing better that she knew, exposed society's preoccupation with the matter of female attractiveness and the cult of womanhood, as imposed and defined by men. She delineated with cutting precision the rewards and penalties that the culture holds out for its own mythologies regarding the obligations of women to be beautiful.

The story "Horsie" records an episode in the life of Miss Wilmarth, a trained baby nurse hired to attend the well-to-do and beautiful Camilla Cruger and her infant daughter. Because of her facial features, Miss Wilmarth becomes an easy target for Mr. Cruger's cruel humor. From the beginning, Gerald Cruger, who nightly took his place opposite Miss Wilmarth at the dinner table while his wife was in confinement, privately referred to the nurse as "Horsie." Although he tried to avoid her face, and her solicitous manners, he became increasingly irritated by her equine appearance. He joked to his wife, "All I say is, nobody has any business to go around looking like a horse and behaving as if it were all right. You don't catch horses going around looking like people, do you?" (p. 261).

Not that he disliked Miss Wilmarth; she was kind, efficient, competent. He only resented her unabashed ugliness, an affront to the studied beauty of his surroundings. Even her attempts to fondle baby Diane, produced discomfort for Gerald: "He could not bear to watch her with the baby in her arms, so acute was his embarrassment at her behavior" (p. 265).

Often, he grimly entertained himself on the way home from his office, by rehearsing the dull and predictable conversations that he knew he would exchange with Miss Wilmarth at the dinner table. In one particular fantasy, he concludes his imaginary conversation with, "Well! will you for God's sake finish your oats, Miss Wilmarth, and let me get out of this?" (p. 261).

Camilla Cruger, Gerald's exquisite wife, who stands in sharp contrast to the unattractive nurse, joins her husband in the constant private jokes about Miss Wilmarth, while pretending kindness in her presence.

One evening, Gerald brings home two handsome young men, who after visiting with the vivacious Camilla, join Gerald and Miss Wilmarth for dinner in what turns out to be a deadly, awkward, and discomforting ordeal. That night "there was no laughter during dinner" (p. 210).

On the eve of Miss Wilmarth's departure, Gerald culminates his hypocrisy by bringing "Horsie" gardenias and extravagantly arranging a limousine ride home for her. As the limousine returns Miss Wilmarth to the dullness of her drab life, she radiates with genuine pleasure in her gifts, gazing lovingly at the white bouquet and comforting herself with the thought that "they might not fade for days. And she could keep the box" (p. 275).

The design of the story revolves around the juxtaposition between Miss Wilmarth and Camilla Cruger. From the outset, Miss Wilmarth is depicted as the typical old maid nurse described in terms of stifling clinical sterility:

> She was tall, pronounced of bone, and erect of carriage; it was somehow impossible to speculate on her appearance undressed. Her long face was innocent, indeed ignorant, of cosmetics, and its color stayed steady. Confusion, heat, or hate caused her neck to flush crimson. Her mild hair was pinned with loops of nicked black wire into a narrow knot, practical to support her little cap, like a charlotte russe from a back shop. (p. 260)

One notes the meticulous selection of details that catalogue Miss Wilmarth's seemingly inexcusable lack of femininity, e.g., a face plainly "ignorant of cosmetics," hair crudely
pinned with "nicked wire," and the preposterous looking cap
that resembled, of all things, a "charlotte russe"[90] (p. 260). Told
in the third person, the narrator quickly maneuvers the reader's
attention to the unattractive, grotesque face, undermining the
mock seriousness of the descriptive tone with comic irony.

> Sometimes, when Miss Wilmarth opened the shiny boxes and care-
> fully grouped the cards, there would come a curious expression
> upon her face. Playing over shorter features, it might almost have
> been one of wistfulness. Upon Miss Wilmarth, it served to per-
> fect the strange resemblance that she bore through the years;
> her face was truly complete with that look of friendly melancholy
> peculiar to the gentle horse. It was not, of course, Miss Wilmarth's
> fault that she looked like a horse. Indeed, there was nowhere to
> attach the blame. But the resemblance remained. (p. 260)

Even her festive dress on the one occasion when she is
invited to socialize with her employers cannot soften the gawky,
unattractiveness in the captious eyes of her beholders:

> She had discarded her linen uniform and put on a frock of dark
> blue taffeta, cut down to a point at the neck and given sleeves
> that left bare the angles of her elbows. Small, stiff ruffles oc-
> curred about the hops, and the skirt was short for its year. It
> revealed that Miss Wilmarth had clothed her ankles in rough-
> ened gray silk and her feet in black, casket shaped slippers, upon
> which little bows quivered as if in lonely terror at the expanse
> before them. She had been busy with her hair; it was crimped
> and loosened, and ends that had escaped the tongs were already
> sliding their pins. All the length of her nose and chin was heavily
> powdered; not with a perfumed dust, tinted to praise her skin,
> but with coarse, bright white talcum. (p. 268)

The angular, antiseptic woman, whose work was so "skilled
and rhythmic" (p. 261) that she hardly disrupted the household, is juxtaposed quite obviously with the charming Mrs.
Camilla Cruger, the dainty, intoxicating epitome of the romantically beautiful American woman.

> She [Camilla] had always been pale as moonlight and had always
> worn a delicate disdain, as light as the lace that covered her breast

. . . Motherhood had not brought perfection to Camilla's loveliness. She had that before. (p. 265)

Is the author's purpose merely to juxtapose the incongruities of the two women in order to praise the loveliness of the one at the expense of the other? Is the disparity between the two women a matter of simple polarities between the desirable and undesirable attributes of females? Is the contradiction entirely comic?

The reader must be careful not to leap to the obvious conclusion that the physically pathetic "Horsie" is the only one who is to be pitied in this story. If Miss Wilmarth is doomed to an incomplete life by her personal unattractiveness, Camilla is cast in a more subtle tragedy. A closer examination of both women is in order.

We turn first to the graceless Miss Wilmarth. In the Edenic Cruger household, the dogged efforts of Miss Wilmarth do not excite the slightest interest or compassion. In this abode of "white satin sofas" (p. 264) and "apricot chaise longues" (p. 265), Miss Wilmarth, the work-horse, is a vile misfit—an anachronism, offensive to the eye and irritating to the sense. Even the other servants refer to her namelessly as "that one" (p. 263).

Since male-determined standards have traditionally placed a high value on feminine beauty, Miss Wilmarth's appearance, despite her abilities, sentences her to the role of the undesirable, a monstrous blight to the household. She is regarded as an ugly "old maid,"[91] expected to demonstrate the proper degree of gratitude for the crumbs of recognition bestowed by the beautiful sovereigns whom she so ably serves.[92] Since Miss Wilmarth has not met the mandatory female "obligation" to be beautiful,[93] socially she must accept her handicap and fit in as best as she can.

Unmarried and modest in her background, we learn she works to support herself, her mother, and her aunt, who live crowded together in a tiny, uncomfortable flat. It appears that her existence is colorless and dismal and that she is bound for a life as the butt of jokes, the object of endless ridicule. Does the author intend for the reader to join in the ridicule of Miss Wilmarth's unfortunate face or to pity her for her bleak existence? Perhaps Parker's deeper intention is to lead us subtly away from the unfortunate creature to her lovely idol, Camilla, the angel in the house.

Ironically, Camilla Cruger, the beautiful little rich girl, is actually no better off than her unattractive counterpart. It is true that back against the passages devoted to depicting Miss Wilmarth's singular repulsiveness, Parker devises such images of Camilla's delicate beauty:

> Her friends gathered, adoring, about the apricot satin chaise longue where Camilla lay and moved her hands as if they hung from heavy wrists; they had been wont before to gather and adore at the white satin sofa in the drawing room where Camilla reclined, her hands like heavy lilies on a languid breeze. (p. 265)

> Every night, when Gerald crossed the threshold of her fragrant room, his heart leaped and his words caught in his throat; but those things had always befallen him at the sight of her. (p. 265)

Just as Miss Wilmarth embodies the stereotype Old Maid myth, Camilla personifies the ideal of beauty, grace, and elegance, the "Galatean" idol.[94] Nevertheless there hovers about Camilla a languid, almost imperceptible dissatisfaction. Her trap is more tender than Miss Wilmarth's, but just as certain. Quite simply, she is bored, bored with the baby, bored with her husband, bored with her beauty, bored with her life.

Less obvious in the passages devoted to the celebration of Camilla's beauty are the hints of Camilla's malaise:

> Her visitors said that Camilla looked lovelier than ever, but they were mistaken. She was as lovely as she had always been. . . . They said how white she was and how lifted above other people; they forgot that she had always been pale as moonlight and had always worn a delicate disdain, as light as the lace that covered her breast. Her doctor cautioned tenderly against hurry, besought her to take recovery slowly—Camilla, who had never done anything quickly in her life. (p. 265)

We note, for example, that though she was extolled as "pale as moonlight," she had always worn a delicate "disdain." The "disdain" provides the first clue to her pervasive tedium. With regard to her post-partum "confinement," another form of entrapment, her doctor "cautioned tenderly against hurry, besought her to take recovery slowly," to which Parker adds the curious ending, "Camilla, who had never done anything quickly in her life." What insight does this statement provide regarding the urgency and importance of Camilla's existence?

When Gerald asks Camilla if "Horsie" rated a night off, Camilla responds, "'Where would she want to go?' Her low, lazy words had always the trick of seeming a little weary of their subject" (p. 264). Is there a deeper inference in the line, "Where would *she* want to go?" (emphasis added) that is linked as much or perhaps more to Camilla than it is to Miss Wilmarth? After all, we may assume that given Miss Wilmarth's humble existence and simple pleasures, there are many places she would "want to go" and hadn't been. Camilla, on the other hand, who appears world-weary and blasé, may indeed have nowhere left "to go." Given this possibility, new meaning is derived from the phrase "her words had always the trick of seeming a little weary of their subject." Is the languid and disdainful Mrs. Cruger "weary" of her own words, and hence of herself?

Ostensibly, Camilla is the radiant new mother of her first child, surrounded by servants, tended to by nurses, adored by friends, indulged by well-to-do parents, and loved by a handsome husband. Yet, in one of the rare moments between the mother and the baby daughter, Camilla relates suspiciously to the child, surprisingly referring to her as "useless" (p. 266).

"Camilla would look at the baby, amusement in her slow glance. 'Good night, useless,' she would say" (p. 266). But there is a gnawing truth behind the jest. In what sense is this, her first-born child, "useless" to Camilla? In rendering joy? Fulfillment? Interest? Meaning to her life? Although the jibe may be merely a parent's casual jest, the reader is tempted to speculate on some deeper implications. Given the suggestions of Camilla's boredom, what if anything would be regard as "useful" in Camilla's exquisitely unhurried eyes?

The reference to "useless" invokes a number of other interesting propositions with regard to women. The child is a daughter, for whom the word "useless" may indeed be an ironic judgment. If Camilla sees herself and her own beautiful vapid life as "useless," then certainly she might make the same prophecy for her daughter,[95] as the female heir to her beauty and her boredom.

On the other hand, the authorial intention in the selection of the child's name, Diane, deserves brief investigation. Diana is the mythological goddess of the moon, and of women in childbirth. Identified with the Greek goddess Artemis, the virgin huntress, and attended by virgins, Diana was protector of women and worshipped by women. Clearly, all of these associations have strong links with a more potent essence of womanhood. In naming the daughter, Diane, the author invests the child with a secret wish that she might validate her womanhood in more assertive terms and avoid being "useless" like her mother, the fragile and delicately named Camilla.

Camilla's exalted life is rooted in inertia. During the course of the story, Camilla herself literally moves only from the apricot-satin chaise longue in the bedroom to the white satin sofa in the drawing room where her hands hung like "heavy lilies in a languide breeze" (p. 265). By contrast, Miss Wilmarth bustles about the house skillfully, efficiently tending to the infant with "big, trustworthy hands, scrubbed and dry" (p. 260) filled with brisk, experienced purpose.

Furthermore, Camilla at one point reminds Gerald that while he is forced to tolerate Miss Wilmarth at dinner, she, on the other hand, must lie around all day while Miss Wilmarth fusses about—not exactly her idea of a "whirl of gaiety, lying here" (p. 264). The references to her "lazy voice" (p. 266) and her "insolent drawl" (p. 269) enhance the image of her listless beauty, but simultaneously contribute to the picture of ennui and tedium in her exquisitely tiresome existence as the reader perceives it. Like the fragile camellia blossom nurtured under glass, doubtless a deliberate correspondence, Camilla Cruger is similarly delicately imprisoned.

Although she has achieved more social acceptability as a "Galatean ideal of beauty, grace and elegance,"[96] Camilla, in very different ways, is just as confined as Miss Wilmarth, who remains trapped in the integuments of her ugly body. In the final analysis, perhaps Parker may be suggesting here that being a woman is to be doomed—whether beautiful or ugly; "Horsie" just happens to provide the technical contrast necessary to the story. Though Camilla may only vaguely sense the subtlety of her entrapment, if indeed she perceives it at all, the author invites the reader to see Camilla's life as useless and wasteful. The story then is a seething indictment of both images projected on women as a result of traditional mythologies.

The role of Gerald Cruger is correspondingly self-centered and lacking in substantive values. Outwardly an adoring and tender husband, Gerald's darker side is marked by petulance and chauvinism. Clearly he resents the birth of his daughter as an intrusion in his life with Camilla.

> He would think, and with small pleasure, of the infant Diane, pink and undistinguished and angry, among the ruffles and *choux* of her bassinet. It was her doing that Camilla had stayed so long away from him in the odorous limbo of the hospital. (p. 263)

His pleasure in his daughter is "small"; he takes umbrage with her presence and shows little fatherly interest in her. Moreover, it is also evident that Gerald's indignation toward the child stems at the moment from the fact that Camilla is denied to him sexually, as a result of her post-delivery condition. "We must take our time" the doctor said, "just ta-a-a-ake our ti-yem" (p. 263), the doctor repeats childishly to Camilla, delivering this piece of medical wisdom with sufficient innuendo. Gerald understands, and vows privately that this inconvenience will never be repeated.

> Yes, well, that would all be because of young Diane. It was because of her, indeed, that night upon night he must face Miss Wilmarth and comb up conversation. All right, young Diane, there you are and nothing to do about it. But you'll be an only child, young woman, that's what you'll be. (p. 263)

We see from the above that Gerald has identified the coming of Miss Wilmarth, the birth of Diane, and his enforced sexual abstinence from his wife, separately and cumulatively, as a source of frustration to his sense of manhood. It is further interesting to note that Gerald's ability to tolerate Miss Wilmarth, the child, and his wife's postpartum confinement would extract a degree of selflessness and understanding from the young husband. His inability to deal intelligently and compassionately with what is obviously a temporary accommodation to all three females, suggests his immaturity and lack of character. Gracious manners notwithstanding, as a sensitive man, Gerald fails abysmally. Indeed he is responsible for perpetuating conventional male projections toward all three women, and sustaining social mythologies of a patriarchal order.

Pursuing the connection between the arrival of Miss Wilmarth and Gerald's enforced sexual abstinence from his wife, it follows that Gerald also links Miss Wilmarth's departure five weeks later with the resumption of sex with Camilla. Hence, the roses he buys for Camilla and the gardenias for MissWilmarth celebrate his own private fertility rite.

Because of Gerald's narrow attitudes toward women, his wife's elegant beauty serves only to elicit from him the most negative qualities, e.g., possessiveness, jealousy, immaturity, as well as the inability to accept fatherhood. "If that brat ever calls you 'Mummy,'" he told Camilla once, "I'll turn her out in the snow" (p. 266). Though apparently said sarcastically as a retaliation to Miss Wilmarth's nightly ritual in which she admonished the baby to say, "Nigh-nigh, 'Mummy" (p. 266), nevertheless the outburst carries its own innuendo hinting at Gerald's darker motives.

The author's juxtaposition of Camilla and Miss Wilmarth as a sardonic reverberation of the myth of beauty and the beast provides opportunity to pursue a moral basis to the story, that is lost to Gerald. The reader perceives that Miss Wilmarth's fatal resemblance to a horse actually appears to increase in proportion to her feelings of rejection by others. Gerald observes that her equine appearance intensifies when she is rebuffed by the maid, and 'though he did not know why, it was the look she sometimes had when she opened the shiny white boxes and lifted the exquisite scentless blossoms that were sent to Camilla" (p. 263). He observes these things, but his careless and insensitive nature cannot assimilate their significance.

It is apparent that the attention lavished on Camilla augments Miss Wilmarth's sense of her own ugliness. The final scene, when Gerald buys "Horsie" gardenias as a parting gift because he was so "crazed at the idea that she was really going" (p. 274), underscores Gerald's limitations.

Clearly the gift has different meanings to each of them. To Miss Wilmarth the gift signifies that she is a person, viewed with feelings and compassion rather than an object regarded merely as useful and functional. Her emotional response horrifies Gerald":

Her squeaks of thanks made red rise back of his ears . . . Gerald was in sudden horror that she might bring her head down close

> to them [the flowers] and toss it back, crying, "wuzza, wuzza, wuzza" at them the while. (p. 272)

He quickly reaffirms the proper social distance, and jokes cruelly to his wife, "Thank the Lord she didn't put them on. I couldn't have stood that sight" (p. 274), and packs Miss Wilmarth off in a taxi. The reader notes that as Miss Wilmarth took her seat in the limousine that Gerald had ordered for her, and thought of Camilla with her "easy young men" and the "shiny white boxes for her, filled with curious blooms," a beholder would have been "startled to learn that a human face could look as much like that of a weary mare as did Miss Wilmarth's" (p. 275). However, as the car swerved,

> The florist's box slipped against Miss Wilmarth's knee. She looked down at it. Then she took it on her lap, raised the lid a little and peeped at the waxy white bouquet. It would have been all fair then for a chance spectator; Miss Wilmarth's strange resemblance was not apparent, as she looked at her flowers. They were her flowers. A man had given them to her. She had been given flowers. They might not fade maybe for days. And she could keep the box. (p. 275.)

Ironically, as she is driven away, there is no one there to notice that her resemblance to the horse has faded. "The strange resemblance" no longer apparent, her long-suffering female role as an ugly and rejected creature is momentarily transformed by the softening effects of her pleasure in Gerald's gift. Though the reader may be tempted to romanticize the miraculous effects of Gerald's gesture and share in Miss Wilmarth's evanescent happiness, an alternative reading is suggested.

Gerald's impetuous act of "thoughtfulness," paradoxically his expression of relief in being liberated from her ugliness, is actually misinterpreted by the pathetic Miss Wilmarth. The gift is given neither in love nor in kindness nor in recognition of her virtues as a human being. While Miss Wilmarth's pleasure is sincere, Gerald's gift is not. As a woman, Miss Wilmarth has gained little. Indeed, Miss Wilmarth's marvelous transformation bears a cruel irony. It symbolizes the easy manipulation of Miss Wilmarth as a woman by the flattery of a false man. We recall that it is not so much the flowers as it was that "a man had given them to her" (p. 275). Miss Wilmarth's human need for recognition is evident, but fraudulently met. Indeed, Parker explicitly holds up Miss Wilmarth for sympathy, even pity. However, the author balances that compassion with irony by implicitly suggesting that Miss Wilmarth, despite her fleeting bliss, has been taken in as a woman by Gerald's spurious recognition.

Miss Wilmarth is still a woman sentenced to imprisonment in the repulsiveness of her own body, carrying with her the shame and guilt inflicted by a world of traditionally defined sexual standards and judgments that can denigrate women for their unattractiveness.

In a society that worships beauty and is obsessed with success and material things, the interior life is fundamentally uninteresting. Hence, it comes as no surprise that neither Gerald nor his wife observe anything about Miss Wilmarth, with the exception that she is unsightly. Prior to her departure, Miss Wilmarth, wishing to avoid any inconvenience over her leaving, remarks that her apartment is only blocks away and that she lives there with her mother.

> Oh, now Gerald had never thought of her having a mother. Then there must have been a father, too, some time. And Miss Wilmarth existed because two people once had love and known. It was not a thought to dwell upon. (p. 273)

Gerald cannot comprehend Miss Wilmarth in human terms as a person who may have been a product of romantic love. Indeed, any reference to human affection from Miss Wilmarth strikes him as discomfiting. Earlier, in response to Miss Wilmarth's cheery attempt to characterize the baby as a potential "heartbreaker," Gerald becomes uneasy. Somehow it "embarrassed him to hear Miss Wilmarth banter of swains and conquest. It was unseemly, as rouge would have been unseemly on her long mouth and perfume on her flat bosom" (p. 264). A plain woman, it would appear, has no right to speak of romantic love, no less desire it.

Despite the Crugers' lack of concern for her, Miss Wilmarth innocently volunteers the information on the day of her departure that in addition to her mother, her aunt lives with her in an apartment that is "a little bit crowded for the three of us—I sleep on the davenport when I'm home, between cases. But it's so nice for Mother, having my aunt there" (p. 273).

Untouched and uninterested, the self-absorbed Crugers later cruelly joke to each other, "That was a fascinating glimpse of her home life she gave us. Great fun." "I don't suppose she minds" (p. 274) concludes Gerald, as through Miss Wilmarth's ugliness were proper grounds for a life of shabbiness and, conversely, only beautiful people had a claim on luxury. The author's ironic indictment of shallow affluent values is blatant and inevitable in an American society in which Mr. and Mrs. Cruger symbolize power, power that is contained in their wealth and beauty and that is used capriciously to serve the demands of their pampered hearts. The image of Camilla in her beautiful home, living luxuriously with her handsome husband and well-tended child seems to reflect society's narrowest vision of success for a woman.

But Camilla Cruger is a participant and perpetuator of the empty values that ultimately and retrospectively have a withering effect on her own life as a woman. Her beauty and affluence do not liberate her or energize her potential. She achieves no insight to enable her to better define herself and her relationship to the outer world, nor does she approach a sense of self-awareness which grows from within. Instead her life corrupts her. We view her as a deficient woman lacking an honest personal moral code—a flawed and stagnant beauty whose dream marriage grants her only the pleasures of the female pursuit of continuing youth and beauty. The hints of her boredom are already evident in her malaise and the reader suspects that her current dream marriage may bear the seeds of a subsequent nightmare.[97] She remains in her fragrant room, the object of her husband's possessive worship, unfulfilled as a mother, untouched as a human being, helpless, bored, indulged, and unaware as a woman.

The reader feels certain that the spiritual impoverishment of Camilla is a far greater defect that the physical impoverishment of Miss Wilmarth. The traditional value placed on women's beauty, ironically permits neither woman the full range of her human potential. Though appearing harmless enough, the charming Gerald Cruger ensures his supremacy, indeed his moral right to power, by making a mythology to substantiate his claim—to one side stands the beautiful Camilla, to the other the bestial Miss Wilmarth. From Gerald's perspective that is all he knows, and all he cares to know. Hence Gerald's ideals of women, derived from a value system based on feminine attractiveness, supply little positive reflection of female potential. From a feminist perspective his view is the troubling embodiment of an attitude that circumscribes a woman's existence by virtue of her physical attributes.

As a satirist, Parker had a talent for seeing what was wrong; she had no special ability for seeking how it should be corrected. It would be easy to conclude that Parker was simply hostile toward the "rich bitches" or the "simpering spinsters"[98] that she portrays, but that would fail to take into account her function as a satirist. What the story confirms is that a woman's identity is in danger when it draws meaning from superficial appearances that embody specious cultural values, and when that identity adopts standard, frequently male models of aesthetic creations as its principal goal.[99] The author's sympathetic portrait of Miss Wilmarth coupled with her ironic gaze at the Crugers also suggests Parker's sensitivity to the serious undercurrents of her text.

Though Parker denounced and mocked the social pretenses and misogyny of the life she perceived as a woman and a writer, she was unable to extricate herself from its effects. By the time the story "Horsie" was published in 1932, Dorothy Parker's private life had become a tawdry burlesque. In addition to her well-known indiscretion with alcohol and drugs, she chose handsome young actors to escort her around town and began dating homosexuals. She was familiar with the distance between the rich and the poor, the cavalier way in which the upperclass treated the working class, the emptiness of elite marriages, and though she abhorred the hypocrisy of it all, she was nevertheless a willing participant.

Between 1930 and 1933, she was reveling in a life that sickened her. As she looked at the indigent on the street, made money and spent it as though she were repulsed by it, and was contemptuous of the young men she gathered about her, she continued to play out her fiction in life and her life in fiction.

Danse Macabre: Female Entrapment:
"The Waltz" (1933)

When Alan Campbell appeared in Parker's life in the spring of 1933, Parker was close to forty, alone, and desperate for a lover. From the start, they were drawn to each other. It was said that Campbell resembled a young Scott Fitzgerald, before drinking had extracted its toll on Fitzgerald's elegant appearance. Parker was immediately impressed by Alan's golden good looks, dazzling smile, high sense of fun, and ebullient, almost adoring personality. The fact that he was twenty-nine, eleven years younger than Dorothy, seemed unimportant to him.

Ironically, and perhaps significantly, they came from the same mixture of Jewish and Gentile background. Both were half Scottish and half Jewish. In Alan's case, his father was of Scotch descent, and his mother's family were Jewish emigres from France. Somehow, word got around that Campbell's father was a wealthy Virginian tobacco tycoon, a mistaken idea that Campbell could never bring himself to correct.

Nevertheless, by the time he met Dorothy, Alan had appeared in several Broadway shows, and had also achieved some success in writing and selling fiction, mostly about life in the theatre. According to Alan, despite the differences in age and personal idiosyncracies, the attraction was mutual and instantaneous. "She was the only woman I ever knew whose mind was completely attuned to mine."[100] They shared many likes and dislikes, but they were especially compatible in their critical judgments.

Alan's mother, Hortense, who had followed him to New York, in order to retrieve him from a wasted life upon the stage, was stunned to find him in a relationship with the celebrated Dorothy Parker, who was only twelve years younger than she. A strikingly handsome, well-built, six-foot-two athletic looking man, Alan had made a surprising reputation playing feminine parts in school productions, a fact which gave rise to rumors regarding his bi-sexuality. Before meeting Dorothy, Alan's involvements with the opposite sex had been with older women, whom he had pampered and treated with gentle, even excessive attention. Though friends agreed that they never saw Campbell do anything overtly homosexual, they also felt that "somewhere in his past, there had been homosexual friendships."[101]

It mattered little to Dorothy what was said or rumored, since it was increasingly clear that Dorothy and Alan were in love, and that their attraction was not only rooted in genuine friendship, but included physical love as well.

They arrived in each other's lives precisely at the moment they most needed each other. Alan faced up to the fact that his acting talent was limited and that his real talent was in writing. With Dorothy at his side, he envisioned the potential of their future together as a writing team, perhaps in Hollywood. Dorothy on the other hand, needed someone to take charge of her life. Apart from his uncritical appreciation of her wit, and his devotion to her as a lover, it was obvious that Alan could also generate harmony and order to a discordant and disheveled domestic existence.

Parker knew nothing of cooking, shopping, cleaning, or keeping track of funds. Often her appearance was less than impeccable, her apartment was in disarray, and her pets were left disobedient and unhousebroken. Alan, a methodically organized and dapper young man, brought neatness, discipline, and a sense of security to her life. He shopped, cooked, painted and redecorated the apartment, cleaned up after the dogs, supervised Dorothy's wardrobe, fussed with her hair, chose her perfume, fixed the cocktails, paid the bills; in all doted on her, amused her and adored her. She cut down on her drinking and disciplined her writing. Donald Ogden Stewart remarked later, "That he took her and probably kept her living."[102] In return for that, Alan claimed to be fully compensated. "No one in the world has made me laugh as much as Dottie.[103]

They were married in New Mexico on June 18, 1933, while Alan played summer stock in Colorado, and Dorothy played Alan's wife in what she referred to as the "first real happiness I've had in my whole life."[104] Though Parker had reason to exult in her marital bliss, the memory of a lonely forty year old woman who had staggered into a costume ball in New York City that previous winter, seeking male companionship, was not far behind her. Misty-eyed from drink and depression, she remembered leaning over the railing of a balcony, looking at the dance floor, muttering in despair, "come on up, anybody,"[105] as the terror of years of emptiness loomed in the distance. Campbell had rescued her from that fate, but Parker knew first hand the pain of solitude and fear of loneliness.

She brought this awareness to the celebrated monologue, "The Waltz,"[106] where she surveyed the comic plight of a single plain middle aged woman with outward characteristic humor, but not without underlying serious emotion.

"The Waltz" is generally regarded as a comic story about a woman and her awkward dancing partner. The setting is a dance, unidentified in nature and unspecified in surroundings. The central conflict rages within the narrator herself, an unnamed woman torn by her social responsibility to her partner on the one hand and her personal hatred for him on the other. A dramatic soliloquy, it portrays the woman's plight when she chooses to dance with a clumsy dance partner rather than remain a wallflower.

The narrator opens the story by accepting an invitation to dance from an anonymous man. "Why, thank you so much. I'd adore to" (p. 47). With that begins the evolution of the woman's cynical thoughts as the dance becomes an excruciating ordeal, both physically and emotionally.

The opening line is a response to a question that has been asked before the story starts and is part of the narrator's external language of the world directed to her dance partner. The next passage introduces the internal language of the self, as the woman realizes, "I don't want to dance with him. I don't want to dance with anybody. And even if I did, it wouldn't be him" (p. 47).

Alternating between external dialogue and internal monologue, "The Waltz" progresses to reveal that not only does the woman grow to resent her dance partner, but she also despises the social conventions she feels have forced her into this position. Her external dialogue continues to reiterate her false ecstasy as she waltzes with her partner, while the internal monologue seethes with anger over the range of indignities to which she is subjected, including his awkwardness as a dance partner, his conduct as a male, and her accommodations as a woman.

Her external comments cover polite small talk regarding the loveliness of the music, her delight in his mastery of the dance, and her rationalizations devised to excuse his persistent lack of grace on the dance floor. "No, of course it didn't hurt.— Why it didn't a bit. Honestly. And it was all my fault" (p. 49), she exclaims at one point, secretly thinking, "two stumbles, slip, and a twenty-yard dash; yes. I've got it. I've got several other things, too, including a split shin and a bitter heart" (p. 50).

As the music draws to a close, the speaker resolves her dilemma on the same false note it had begun. She instructs her partner: "Do tell them to play this same thing. I'd simply adore to go on waltzing" (p. 51).

Married to an actor, attending theatre regularly, writing theatre criticism, and associating at the Algonquin with performers, producers, and playwrights, Parker was heavily influenced by writing for the stage. Nowhere is that clearer than in the monologue, "The Waltz." The juxtaposition of the private and public voice of the narrator is the major structural device of the story as well as the source of its humor, but more importantly keys us into the personal and private hell of the speaker. The opening line of the story, "Why, thank you so much. I'd adore to" (p. 47), is italicized, presumably spoken aloud. It is followed by an interior monologue, not italicized, which contradicts what has just been said:

> I don't want to dance with him. I don't want to dance with anybody. And even if I did it wouldn't be him. He'd be well down among the last ten. I've seen the way he dances; it looks like something you do on Saint Waldurgis Night. Just think, not a quarter of an hour ago, here I was sitting, feeling so sorry for the poor girl he was dancing with. And now I'm going to be the poor girl. Well, well. Isn't it a small world? (p. 47)

Publicly she claims she "adores" the waltz; privately she compares the dance to "something you do on Saint Waldurgis Night," the high night of evil, the witches' sabbath. Distraught and miserable, the protagonist launches secretly into a private volley of mock self-assessments, her true version of her relationship to her partner. "My name . . . stands for Despair, Bewilderment, Futility, Degradation and Premeditated Murder" (p. 47).

How does one reconcile the serious and the comic elements of this work? It may be simply stated that "The Waltz" is a humorous story with a serious theme. On the surface, the triviality of the situation, i.e., a woman and her clumsy dance partner bravely struggling through a waltz, seems plainly funny. However, another reading is offered in this study which suggests the unseen horror of the protagonist's existence as an older woman, trapped in a savage and deadly relationship with a man she reviles. At its core, the story serves as an emblematic study of women and their relationship to men.

We turn to the formal contrast between the inner and outer voice for a closer examination of the structure and language, as an entry into the narrator's female sensibility. Structurally the dichotomy between the inner and outer dialogue reflects the speaker's conflict between the desire to disguise and the desire to disclose. Graphically, the story begins and ends in italicized speech. Covering only five pages, seven short italicized speeches of external monologue alternate with six longer unitalicized speeches of internal dialogue. What the narrator thinks is given considerably greater attention than what she says.

The opening line establishes the traditional sexual roles: a female response to a male offer. But what is he offering? What is it she would 'adore" to do? Only as we enter her private thoughts in the second line do we understand that what she says she would adore to do is to dance with him. Yet, at that precise moment, we discover simultaneously that the one thing she would really not adore to do—is to dance with him. This construct of accommodation and contradiction is built in from the outset and maintained throughout the soliloquy.

Though the story is presented entirely in the first person, "I," the narrator is both literally and metaphorically a divided being. The initial information that the reader receives, "Why, thank you so much. I'd adore to," is brief, polite, and conventionally feminine. The private voice revealed in the next long descriptive passage is marked by rough comic savagery filled with reference to physical pain: "All right, Cannonball, let's run out on the field. You won the toss; you can lead" (p. 48).

Sheila Graham once commented of Parker, "This was Dottie, nice to your face, cruel behind your back. The only way she could live with herself was to murder everybody else with biting words."[107] This divided behavior, coaxing friendship of someone and later attacking him, was precisely the structural and linguistic format that found expression in the two voices of the narrator in "The Waltz."

The personality of the speaker and her position in the story revolve around this narrative device of double consciousness, which not only distinguished between what the narrator says and what she thinks, but also illuminates other features of the story relating to women's speech and "verbal subversion."[108] The narrator, actively involved in the events, reports the story from a point in time after the experience itself. Her angle of perspective is idiosyncratic; it remains fixed at the center of her experiences, limited to her own thoughts, feeling, and perceptions. Yet the advantage of this point of view is that it creates immediacy and intimacy.

While the reader is allowed to cross the boundaries between the contradictions of the inner monologue and the outer dialogue, the male partner on the other hand has access only to the narrator's outer voice and is not privileged to speak at all. The outer voice is stereotypically feminine and manifests most of the characteristics of what Robin Lakoff attributes to "women's language"[109]—drawing heavily on what is termed "ladylike" language.[110]

For example, "The Waltz" provides numerous examples of trivializing words like "adore" and "thrilled" and intensifiers like "simply," "really," "truly," and "so." The narrators's public language is thick with adverbs and adjectives as well as tag questions and repetitions that mark acquiescence and accommodations. "It's lovely, isn't it? She says repeatedly, "Isn't it? It's simply lovely. It's the loveliest waltz, isn't it?" (p. 49). Her speech is rife with "feminine" particles, such as "oh" throughout; "Oh, yes" (p. 48), "Oh, no, no, no" (p. 48), "Oh, goody" (p. 50), "Oh darn" (p. 51).

An instructive method of observing the characteristics of this public female language in context, is to cite the seven short passages of italicized external dialogue separately and chronologically as they appear in the story:

I. Why thank you so much. I'd adore to. (p. 47)

II. Why, I think it's more of a waltz, really, isn't it? We might just listen to the music a second. Shall we? Oh yes, it's a waltz, Mind? Why I'm simply thrilled. I'd love to waltz with you. (p. 48)

III. Oh, no, no, no. Goodness no. It didn't really hurt the least little bit. And anyway it was my fault. Really it was. Truly. Well you're just being sweet, to say that. It really was all my fault.

IV. Yes, it's lovely, isn't it. It's simply lovely. It's the loveliest waltz. Isn't it? Oh, I think it's lovely too. (p. 49)

V. No. Of course it didn't hurt. Why, it didn't hurt a bit. Honestly. And it was all my fault. You see, that little step of yours—well it's perfectly lovely, but it's just a tiny bit tricky to follow at first. Oh, did you work it up yourself? You really did? Well, aren't you amazing! Oh now I think I've got it. Oh, I think it's lovely. I was watching you do it when you were dancing before. It's awfully effective when you look at it. (p. 50)

VI. Oh, they've stopped. The mean things. They're not going to play anymore. Oh darn, Oh, do you think they would? Do you really think so if you gave them twenty dollars? Oh that would be lovely. And look, do tell them to play this same thing. I'd simply adore to go on waltzing. (p. 51)

In these seven spoken passages of twenty-four lines, the combination of the words "sweet," "adore," and variants of "lovely" are used twelve times, virtually in every other line. With the exception of two instances, both meant in sarcasm: "I'd *love* to waltz with you. I'd love to have my tonsils out" (emphasis added; p. 48) and later, a mockery of her disgust for the man, "I couldn't bear to have anything happen to him. I love him. I love him . . . Ow! Get off my instep you hulking peasant! (p. 49), there are no other references to or variants of the word "love" in the remaining 146 lines of internal monologue.

Presented as a verbal repertoire specifically shaped to the presence of a male, the narrator's external, lady-like dialogue is content-free—devoid of meaning, thought, opinion, and depth. It certainly lacks truth. Replete with monotony, fawning accommodations and overly polite euphemisms, the language is flowery, tentative, qualified and apologetic. As a woman the speaker repeatedly places herself in a publicly subordinate role to her male partner, while she rages inwardly at his stupidity: "It was all my fault. You see, that little step of yours—well, it's perfectly lovely, but it's just a tiny bit tricky to follow at first" (p. 49). Furthermore, she is unable to admit honestly to either fatigue or stress, and rather than forgo her adaptive image she insists, "It didn't hurt the least little bit" (p. 48) and "Tired? I should say I'm not tired" (p. 50).

In her discussion of power in a literary text, Barbara Bellow Watson suggests that the language of women may also reflect another kind of conscious "protective accommodation" that conceals whatever power of knowledge the speaker may actually possess.[111] Hence, when the speaker says, "Why, I think it's more of a waltz, really, isn't it?" (p. 48), she appears to be asking for information when in reality she is concealing what she knows and is really giving information. Because she fears alienating those whom she has been conditioned to believe are the true possessors of power and knowledge, the female speaker disguises her knowledge in deferential style.

In the shallow dullness of the spoken dialogue, we recognize a dual irony. The author satirizes the way women are "supposed to talk," not necessarily how they should or even do talk. The reader cannot fail to grasp the flip-side meaning, which presents us with a male caricature as well, who silently, presumably agreeably (if one takes the outcome of the story as an indicator) accepts these silly superficialities as the way women really do and should talk. "The exaggerated language of the speaker in 'The Waltz' is socially impeccable and irreproachably 'feminine'; but it is totally false," in effect a caricature of polite women's language. The hypocrisy of the public voice is immediately subverted[112] after each utterance, as the woman perceives that she is trapped "like a trap in a trap"[113] (p. 47), the emblem of her helpless inner rage.

Indeed, throughout the interior monologue, the language is repeatedly marked by images of violence: "When you kick me in the shin, smile" (p. 49); disease: "it's so nice to meet a man who isn't a scaredy-cat about catching my beri-beri" (p. 48); and death: "being struck dead would look like a day in the country, compared to struggling out a dance with this boy" (p. 47).

We know that in her own life, Parker became viciously adept at the game of "embrace-denounce," which she cleverly translated to her work. The external, deceptive charm followed by "behind the back denunciation of almost comic violence" (as described by her friend Lillian Hellman), were practically a blueprint for the split condition of the speaker.[114]

In addition, the shallow, empty chatter of the external dialogue is replaced in this private soliloquy with a wide and sophisticated range of topics that freely make references to sports: "All right, Cannonball, let's run out on the field. You won the toss" (p. 48); history: "Anybody who isn't waltzing with this

Mrs. O'Leary's cow I've got here is having a good time" (p. 50); literature: "I must look like something out of the 'Fall of the House of Usher'" (p. 50); foreign expressions, "*danse macabre*" (p. 51); and to psychoanalysis: "Freud says there are no accidents" (p. 49).

Unlike the self-effacing coquetry of the public voice, the internal voice is punctuated with slang: "We're going on like this, Double-Time Charlie and I" (p. 50); tough talk: "I'll see you in hell first" (p. 48); dialect: "Probably he grew up in the hill country, and never had no 'larning'" (p. 49); and trendy colloquialisms: "A true little corker" (p. 47). Interesting, smart, funny, the private voice of the narrator crackles with vitriolic wit and high spirits. The narrator does not hesitate privately to clarify her partner as "Mr. Jukes"[115] (p. 47), an "idiot" (p. 48), "a hulking peasant" (p. 49), "butch" (p. 49), "Cannonball" (p. 48), while at the same time she mockingly denigrates herself as "something out of the Fall of the House of Usher" (p. 50) suffering with "beri-beri" (p. 48), and exhibiting symptoms of "Despair, Bewilderment, Futility, Degradation and Premeditated Murder" (p. 47) as though her associations with this sinister partner have had a corruptive effect on her.

Admittedly, she notes of herself privately in the third monologue: "I've led no cloistered life" (p. 49), despite the professed innocence of her public dialogue on the dance floor. However, this particular phrase is more than a reproach. It signals a pivotal shift in tone that leads the reader to a more malicious level beyond the bounds of social sarcasms and wisecracking witticism into something that resembles stark hatred and sexual violence.

The narrator continues: "I've known dancing partners who have spoiled my slippers and torn my dress; but when it comes to kicking, I am Outraged Womanhood" (p. 49). The associative connotations are unmistakably sexual. Preceded by the reference to Freud, who says that "there are no accidents" (p. 49), added to her references to the unwholesome Jukes, his "degenerate cunning" (p. 50), and later to "What do you think I am, anyway—a gangplank? Ow!" (p. 49), the waltz carries with it the metaphoric itinerary of sexual abuse. The references to "I hate this creature" (p. 48), to his movements as a *danse macabre*, and to her suggestion that "I'll just lie low, and watch the pace of him" (p. 48) and finally most provocatively, her hysterical outcry, "I am Outraged Womanhood" (p. 49—designated in capital letters—) all invoke a note of feminine violation as the waltz becomes a metaphor for rape. I've had partners "who have spoiled my slippers" (p. 49) suggests sexual besmirchment. New resonance is derived from the phrase "Die he must and die he shall, for what he did to me" (p. 48). In this context the language of the internal episode is explicitly shocking, and the cleverness, exaggeration, and verbal play that have disguised the speaker's bitter voice surface with a vengeance. The charade is over.

Coupled with the earlier names the speaker gave herself, i.e. "Despair, Bewilderment, Futility, Degradation," her outburst as "Outraged Womanhood" bestows an almost archetypal quality on the parade of unnamed females at dances and other rituals of social intercourse that serve to humiliate women. Thus, the ostensible contrast between the spoken dialogue and the internal monologue takes no further significance with regard to the thematic impressions of the story as a view of women.

The fifth monologue is unequivocal—unpretentious. The impudent wit ceases. The humor, deadly and unadorned, seethes with unrestrained malevolence.

> I hate this creature I'm chained to. I hated him from the moment I saw his leering, bestial face. And here I've been locked in his noxious embrace for the thirty-five years this waltz has lasted. Is that orchestra never going to stop playing? Or must this obscene travesty of a dance go on until hell burns out? (p. 50)

Churning with venom and bitterness, the speaker has translated the waltz into mortal and sexual combat. "I hate this creature I'm chained to" is thick with suggestive possibilities and shadowy meanings. The male partner has become a "creature." The embrace is "noxious," "obscene." Clearly the waltz has become a living death.

The portrait of the waltz, with its harsh images of sexual assault and embattled fury against male dominion, has also at its core—a vision of death.[116] The narrator observes of the episode itself: "I didn't know what trouble was, before I got down into this *danse macabre* (p. 51). Paula Treichler argues that early entrapment metaphors that occur in the first monologue represent this vision of death. "But what could I do" the speaker asks. "Everyone else at the table had got up to dance, except him and me. There was I, trapped. Trapped like a trap in a trap"[117] (p. 47). The invitation to dance prefigures the symbolic entrapment of her own death. Just as she is verbally trapped and physically trapped, she is socially trapped by male cultural imperatives that complete her purgatory. The "obscene travesty of a dance" is linked to the fires of "hell"; she is "aching," "chained," "locked" (p. 50) in a terrifying death trap that suffocates her.

At one point in the crucial fifth monologue, the narrator remarks: "This sort of thing takes a fearful toll of a woman my age" (p. 50). What is her age? What is her social status? How old is her partner? A clue may be found in re-examining the passage that follows:

> Yes I've got it. I've got several other things too, including a split shin and a bitter heart. I hate this creature I'm chained to. I hated him the moment I saw his leering bestial face. And here I've been locked in his noxious embrace for the thirty-five years this waltz has lasted. (p. 50)

Assuming that "The Waltz" may be viewed as a microcosm of the narrator's relationship with men, the "thirty five" years may suggest the actual time the partner has spent as a woman "chained" to the "noxious embrace" of a specific creature. Is it necessarily the partner? Perhaps not. It appears that the male dancing partner is of college age. The speaker's age, though older, is less clear. Until now the partner has repeatedly been referred to in boyish terms, a clumsy young athlete: "Cannonball" (p. 48), "Triple Threat," "He is youth and vigor and courage" (p. 49). However, at this explosive moment, the narrator's psychic probings seem to involve more than this boy and this dance. She plumbs a deeper well of collected memories touching a stored recollection of her accumulated life as a woman: "Yes I've got it. I've got several other things too, including a split shin, and a bitter heart" (p. 50). What does she mean by "several other things"? How long has she had a "bitter heart"? The comic reference to the immediate "split shin" does not neutralize the impact of the "other things," wounds from another time and place, perhaps; nor does it obfuscate the allusion to what appears to be a chronic "bitter heart." Is the narrator suggesting that she has a "bitter heart" for the "thirty-five years" that she has literally been "chained" to another man, her husband? Or perhaps to some generalized representation of all men, who have forced her into the self-deceptions that engendered a bitter heart for a lifetime of thirty-five years?[118]

The plausibility of the latter revolves around the reader's ability to bestow archetypal, almost figural qualities to the pronoun "his" in the phrase, "I've been locked in *his* noxious embrace for the thirty-five years this waltz has lasted" (emphasis added). In either case, her imprisonment appears to enclose her in a terrifying cycle of physical, psychological, and verbal bondage.

The last monologue draws together metaphors of death and heavenly rebirth. It begins: "I should say I'm not tired. I'm dead, that's all I am. Dead" (p. 50). The image of the narrator, waltzing through eternity with "Double-time Charlie," is set against the fleeting memories of her life as it passes before her: "There was the time I was in a hurricane in the West Indies, there was the day I got my head cut open in a taxi smash" (p. 51). The silence, like the "sound of angel voices," signals the end of the waltz and presumably the end of her ordeal. But the last dialogue states otherwise:

> Oh, they've stopped, the mean things. They're not going to play anymore. O, darn. O do you think they would? Do you really think so if you gave them twenty dollars? Oh, that would be lovely. And look do tell them to play this same thing. I'd simply adore to go on waltzing. (p. 51)

Doomed to repeat the cycle of her social and sexual entrapment, she pronounces her own death sentence and voluntarily continues her servitude. We return in the last lines to the echo of the first. The narrator's compliance and hypocrisy seem a betrayal. Why does she offer to renew the partnership and go on dancing? She is not trapped as she was at the beginning of the story when "everyone else at the table had got up to dance, except him and me" (p. 47). Certainly from the internal monologue it would appear she has had enough. Is the explanation of a literal surprise ending sufficient to explain the implications? What deeper intention is signified by the narrator's fi-

nal words and action? Embedded in the comic surprise ending is a trenchant irony.

As the final lines lapse into the familiar duplicities, the
speaker squarely faces the grim reality of the male-empowered
hierarchy she has so maligned. She adopts the self-effacing female language of survival and clings to her male partner, as
she knows she must, affirming in the last analysis that the dance
is life.

As a reminder of the economic subordination of the narrator, the male partner pays the musician "twenty dollars" to
play again at her request. She has thus manipulated her partner
to at least extract a price for her pain. Her continued alliance
with her partner as the same music renews itself at her suggestion signifies her awareness of, and resignation to perpetuating the only social role as a woman open to her in the ritual of
interaction. She must go on dancing. The waltz is endless.

Perhaps no other story incarnates, both in style and content, so much of Parker's genius to at once reveal and conceal.
The cloak of comedy did little to disguise the realities of female rage engendered by accommodations to please men.

Though Parker lived smartly among men, depending on
her wise-cracking wit and repartee, to earn her place, in a sense,
she gained and maintained her reputation because she was a
woman who knew how to act like a man and talk like a man. In
a reverse irony she must have recognized, Parker was empow-
ered by her resignation to a patriarchal environment. She saw
in the unnamed narrator of the story a hidden part of herself,
and expressed in the scathing monologue, great artistic empathy as well as a profound emotional alliance with women, for
whom the uneasy waltz is the ceremonial dance between the
sexes.

Women Without Men: " 'Love's Labour's Lost' ": "Glory in the Daytime" (1933)

In the fall of 1933, George Kaufman and Moss Hart, once members of the now defunct Roundtable, mounted their new play,
Merrily We Roll Along, in New York. It featured a wise-cracking
alcoholic woman who was tough, smart, and talked like a man.
According to the story, the fresh and beautiful young Julia

gradually dissipates through the years, ultimately ending up physically sodden, seldom sober, and preferring to sleep with younger men. The theatrical counterpart to Parker was harsh, obvious, and infuriating. Parker had never cared for Kaufman; now she despised him and his literary circle of theatre friends. Alan Campbell seized the moment to propose an escape from New York and its present indignities. Campbell longed for a career as a film writer, and was well aware of Dorothy's value to his ambitions. He asked Dorothy to marry him, planned a honeymoon in California and then swept his new wife off to life in Hollywood.

From the beginning, Dorothy distrusted Hollywood. Nevertheless, Alan and Dorothy signed high-paying contracts as a husband and wife team and turned out ultimately to complement each other's, work. Together, they received screen credits for fifteen films. Dorothy's reputation as a writer at one time earned her $5,200 a week, but to her the work was as empty and banal as were the people. She believed they were living in "Babylonian captivity working for cretins."[119] Despite Alan's industriousness and enthusiasm about their work Parker was depressed that her scripts were actually a composite, written by several writers, and that in reality "she was giving a real gloss to false pearls."[120] She vowed to give Hollywood six months. She hated the sham, the Hollywood rich and she desperately missed New York. As she told Marion Capron, "I can't talk about Hollywood. It was a horror to me when I was there and it's a horror to look back on".[121]

Indeed, the Hollywood years, between 1933 and 1936 were tumultuous. Parker and Alan quarreled more frequently, their drinking grew worse, her language more obscene, her attempted suicides more frequent. Her miscarriage during her third month of pregnancy at the age of forty-two ended their momentary happiness at the prospect of parenthood, and increased the strain between them. Ultimately, she turned against Alan cruelly abusing him as she had Edwin Parker.

However, it was during her first year in Hollywood that "Glory in the Daytime"[122] appeared in print. It reflected the same sham and pretenses of theatrical life in New York that Parker abhorred in Hollywood. The work explores the anguish in the lives of three women. Mrs. Murdock, a naive stagestruck fan is invited for tea by Hallie Noyes, the flamboyant newcomer to the Bridge Club. She promises to introduce "Tiny One," as Miss Noyes called her, to the great actress Lily Wynton.

Thrilled at the prospect of meeting the glamorous figure, Mrs. Murdock enthusiastically treats her husband to every detail of the invitation. His indifference and joking cynicism spoil her anticipated pleasure and arouse her resentment. They dined that night "not in silence, but in pronounced quiet" (p. 279). Throughout the evening, Mrs. Murdock secretly fantasizes her future conversations: "I saw Lily Wynton at Hallie's the other day, and she was telling me all about her new play . . . I had a long letter from Lily Wynton . . . Lily Wynton told me . . . Lily, I said to her . . ." (p. 279).

The next day, filled with the recollections of Lily Wynton "as a tall and silvery presence" (. 276), Mrs. Murdock joins Miss Noyes and Lily Wynton in what turns out to be a disappointing and confusing experience. Lily, past her prime and slightly tipsy at her arrival, swills down brandy, fractures Shakespeare, and drinks to exhaustion, despite Hallie Noyes's efforts to keep her sober for the evening performance. The great actress speaks disparagingly of men, refers incessantly and inaccurately to Mrs. Murdock as a writer, and complains of gas and acidity through the afternoon.

In one particularly startling response to Lily's persistent pleas for more liquor, Miss Noyes remarks: "Do you want me to do what I had to last time. . . Do you want me to strike you, in front of tiny one, here?" (p. 286).

On the way home, Mrs. Murdock, reflecting over her experience, finds herself thinking tenderly of her husband, Jim. Glamour and romance, she concludes, "were right at home all the time" (p. 289). Mrs. Murdock goes out of her way to buy Jim's favorite treats, red caviar and a large, foreign cheese, and plans a "secret party to celebrate her return to contentment with her Jim" (p. 289). Her eyes "a-light" with excitement, she is met by the same caustic references to Hallie Noyes that had dimmed the light in her eyes the day before. From behind his paper, Jim says as she enters, "What did you do? Did you drop up to Hank Noyes?" His reference to Hallie as "Hank" and his sarcastic innuendo about "dropping up" (p. 289) humiliate and confuse her. Degraded by his insensitivity, Mrs. Murdock wearily leaves the room, instructs the maid to put her purchases away for some other time, and pathetically, "little Mrs. Murdock went on down the door of her bedroom" (p. 290) and her disappointments.

Drawing from her adventures amidst the Bohemian lifestyle of an ostentatious and sometimes garish artistic community, Parker found equivalents in the aging actress and the flamboyant lesbian who dominated the pages of the story. The star-struck little woman, disappointed in the phony glamour and empty sordidness of the heralded tea party, nevertheless, earned Parker's sympathy and seemed to echo some of the author's own ambivalent feelings for the fake and artificial world that simultaneously attracted and disturbed her as an artist.

Told in the third person narrative, "Glory in the Daytime" is related through the myopic vision of Little Mrs. Murdock, whose innocent naivete is juxtaposed against the aggressive dominance of Hallie Noyes and the superficial self-centeredness of Lily Wynton. Into the luminous world of eccentricities and histrionics, wistful Mrs. Murdock makes her tentative entrance. However, prior to her involvement in that coterie of females, to which we shall return, Mrs. Murdock plays the quiet, undramatic role of the ordinary wife to an insensitive, albeit realistic, husband.

The story is divided into three major scenes. The first scene portrays the relationship between Mr. and Mrs. Murdock and the agitated discussion of the invitation to tea. The second, long scene depicts the dramatic details of the afternoon tea shared by the three women, and the third scene returns Mrs. Murdock to her home and her husband. Each of the scenes offers the reader a distinctive view of women, who despite their differences and stations in life, ultimately are bonded by the pain they have come to feel toward men.

The opening line of the story provides the first clue to the saga of the Murdocks and their tenuous relationship.

> Mr. Murdock was one who carried no enthusiasm for plays and their players, and that was too bad, for they meant so much to little Mrs. Murdock. (p. 276)

Mr. Murdock's lack of "enthusiasm for plays and players" might appear innocent enough were it not for the second reference to Murdock's response to his wife's invitation to tea.

Mr. Murdock was already at home when she arrived. It required but a glance to tell that for him there had been no signing starts that evening in the heavens. He sat with his newspaper opened at the financial page, and bitterness had its way with his soul. . .Mr. Murdock did not like Miss Noyes. When pressed for a reason, he replied that he just plain didn't like her. Occasionally he added, with a sweep that might have commanded a certain admiration, that all those woman made him sick. (p. 277)

In this passage the reader is provided with important insight into Mr. Murdock's personality. We note that his newspaper is opened at the "financial page," a clue to his unartistic and blunted disposition. Furthermore, we learn that "bitterness had its way with his soul." Clearly the juxtaposition of little Mrs. Murdock, who walked home through the early dark "and stars sang in the sky above her" (p. 277), with Jim, who sat with his "newspaper opened at the financial page, and bitterness had its way with his soul," focuses on the essential contrast that permeates their incompatible relationship. Mrs. Murdock is an emotionally starved housewife in search of glamour and romance. Her wistful worship of all the "free passionate elect who serve the theater" (p. 276) is met by her husband's generalized crusty view "that all those women made him sick."

Yet conditioning and culture have taught Mrs. Murdock her proper female role of accommodator and "angel in the house,"[123] in the ritual games of marriage. The subtle pressure on Mrs. Murdock to resign herself to pathetic ordinariness and angelic submissiveness is an extension of the long-held view challenged by contemporary feminists that "man must be pleased; but him to please/Is women's pleasure."[124] The withering effect of this authoritative repression on the romantic ebullience of Mrs. Murdock is predictable.

However, in the spirit and art of pleasing men, which is not only angelic but in more worldly terms "the proper acts of a lady,"[125] Mrs. Murdock knows "it was not the time to cry happily to him at the impending hospitalities of Miss Noyes; not the time, that is if one anticipated exclamatory sympathy." Furthermore she found, that keeping any mention of Miss Noyes from her accounts of her bridge club meetings "made for a more agreeable evening" (p. 277), and dutifully she did so.

However, on this day, Mrs. Murdock's enthusiasm overcomes her customary obeisance and with shining eyes she repeats the details of Hallie Noyes's invitation to "drop up" (p. 278) for tea and meet Lily Wynton. Jim's response to her excitement is to joke, cruelly: "Drop up . . . How can you drop up?" Later he would repeat disparagingly: "You might ask her how she'd like to try dropping down, for a change" (p. 278). Despite her efforts to share her genuine pleasure with her husband, Mr. Murdock's continued mockery of Mrs. Murdock's almost childlike excitement succeeds in spoiling her exuberance. Her energy drained, we note she walked "wearily" to the door, withdrew to her bedroom with "no light in her eyes" (p. 278).

Later during dinner she retreated from the sterility of their silence to her own luxurious inner thoughts as they ate in "pronounced quiet" (p. 279). Mrs. Murdock surrenders and withdraws into her fantasies. In this manner the author furnishes the reader with the initial glimpse into Mrs. Murdock's inner depths as a married woman.

Mr. Murdock's personal view of women has thus far revealed two qualities, namely, a singular distaste for and impatience with his wife's enthusiasm and romantic imagination and a blatant disgust for her female friends whom he not only dislikes but who he alleges made him "sick" (p. 277). We leave him at the end of the evening as Mrs. Murdock left him earlier, "with only his newspaper and his bitterness for company" (p. 278).

"The next morning, Mr. Murdock had left for his office before Mrs. Murdock rose," a rare event that happened only several times before, Mrs. Murdock recalled, "but not often," and Mrs. Murdock "felt a little queer about it" (p. 279). This passing reference to Mr. Murdock's idiosyncratic behavior, a subtle insight, adds to the growing portrait of Murdock's demeaning and disdainful treatment of his wife.

In the next scene, which dominates the story in length and detail, Mrs. Murdock appears at tea with Hallie Noyes and Lily Wynton. In these passages, devoted to the ironic implications of the title, "Glory in the Daytime," the author explores the pain of all three women. Does Parker's view of these women emanate from the cynical and fecund reservoir of a writer's satiric vision of absurdly "stereotypical females"? Or does the satire mask a more poignant study of hidden hurts and adaptive female behavior? For clarification, we turn to an examination of each of the woman as they interact with each other in the absence of men but responding nevertheless to the inescapability of their experiences with men.

The author's careful attention to the details of the women's wardrobe as they gather that afternoon, provides the first field of contrasting forces at work in the lives of these woman. Dressed in her prim frock of "dark blue serge, with fluted white muslin about the neck and the wrists" (p. 279), the pert little Mrs. Murdock stands in sharp contrast to the masculine Miss Noyes, in her "black velvet trousers, a red cummerbund, and white silk shirt, opened at the throat," a cigarette clinging to her lower lip, and her eyes, "as were her habit, . . . held narrow against its near smoke." Of Mrs. Murdock, Hallie remarks, "Good Lord, you look easily eleven years old in that dress" (p. 280). Although Lily Wynton hovers in Mrs. Murdock's consciousness as a "tall and silvery presence" (p. 276) and appears "just as she should have, in black satin sables and long white gloves" (p. 282), she is clearly past her prime, her figure thick with age, her eyes puffy, and her face sagging. The large black hat with a great soft plume curling across her throat completed the appropriately outlandish outfit. Histrionics notwithstanding, it was "romance . . . it was mystery, . . . it was Lily Wynton's hat and no other would dare it" (p. 282), thought Mrs. Murdock, and it was enough, she argued to herself, to obviate the disturbing facts that Lily's hair had the "various lines of neglected brass" (p. 283) and that embedded in the folds of her glove and the length of her gown were small "bits of food or drops of drink, or perhaps both" (p. 282).

Parker actually recounted to Marion Capron a similarly disturbing moment in Beverly Hills when she saw a "cadillac about a block long, and out of the side windows was a wonderful slinky mink, an arm, and at the end of the arm a hand in a white suede glove wrinkled about a wrist, and in the hand was a bagel with a bite out of it."[126] For Dorothy it symbolized the tacky tastelessness of the film capitol.

As the afternoon wears on it becomes clear that Lily Wynton's life is far from the glorious romance Mrs. Murdock had fantasized. As Lily Wynton herself later confesses, between gulps of brandy and complaints of acidity: "My life . . . is a mess. A stinking mess. It always has been, and it always will be" (p. 285).

Her search for the rich and the famous has led Mrs. Murdock to the garish, pretentious, and unhappy lives of two women who have locked themselves in as painful and unattractive an alliance as her own marriage. An exploration of the association between Lily and Hallie reveals a cumulative picture of misanthropy, lesbianism, sadism, and shared disappointments.

The reader derives the first evidence of both Hallie Noyes's hatred of men and her apparent homosexuality from Hallie's initial observations about Lily's male lovers and her physical attention to Mrs. Murdock as the two await Lily's arrival. "Men. She never had a man that wasn't a louse. . .A pack of lice, always. All of them. Leave her for the first little floozie that comes along" (p. 281), she tells Mrs. Murdock, venting her initial outburst against males. Then, in suggestive gestures too obvious to ignore, Hallie, as she passes Mrs. Murdock and made her way to the door, "stopped suddenly, cupped her guest's round chin and quickly, lightly kissed her mouth" (p. 282). The "sudden" stop and unexpected kiss leave little Mrs. Murdock puzzled, but unsuspecting.

The reader is also struck by Hallie Noyes's presumably artistic preoccupation with modeling torsos of Eve: "I always do Eve. What else is there to do?" as well as her provocative invitation to the innocent Mrs. Murdock to come and pose for her some time, followed by the flirtatious emphasis: "ye-es, you'd be very nice to do. My tiny one" (p. 281). Miss Noyes's flashy behavior and pseudo-affectations, like "designing her own pajamas, or reading Proust, or modeling torsos in plasticine" (p. 277) had the decided effect of forced artiness and ostentation. Her life, like her surname, "Noyes," was showy filled with sound and frivolous motion, but artificially aggressive, devoid of either quiet meaning or genuine warmth. Hallie effected a superficial and immediate sense of intimacy, which was in reality a form of hypocritical aloofness. Condescending and insincere, Hallie's conversation was marked by gushing gaiety and laced with ritual banalities and pompous phrases. "Come in, come in, Tiny One," she said. "Bless its little heart. Take off its little coat . . . Sit ye doon, here beside me. There'll be a spot of tea in a jiff." The linguistic affectations in the assumed dialect: "Sit ye, doon," the silly appellation of Miss Murdock as "Tiny One." the reference to a mature woman in the neuter gender as "it," an indefinite pronoun, in addition to the flippant mockery of women's speech in the repeated allusion to "little coat" and "little heart" (p. 280) create a contemptuous linguistic atmosphere of superiority which Mrs. Murdock is patiently forced to endure. In this sense, the assumed superiority of the masculine Miss Noyes is no less abusive than the cynical snickering of the bitter Mr. Murdock.

Like her living room with its "oblique lines and acute angles" and zigzags of aluminum, mirrors, sawdust, and steel, lacking wood and comfortable seats, Hallie's personality was dazzling for "a visit" (p. 280) but far from conducive to wholesome accommodations.

Awaiting the bedraggled and beguiling Lily Wynton, the androgynous Hallie Noyes was a study in planned Bohemian carelessness. Parker's sardonic juxtaposition of the innocent Mrs. Murdock and the imposing Miss Noyes draws from two antithetical female stereotypes who become linked in their quest for romantic experience in the person of a third stereotype, Lily Wynton. However, Mrs. Murdock's childish adoration of the great actress and Miss Noyes's lesbian relationship with her are met by Lily Wynton's absorbing self-love, which has failed to bring her fulfillment as well. At this level, then, the story penetrates beneath each female stereotype to disclose the pervasive emptiness of all their lives and signals the lack of essentiality in their existence, despite their differences. Even cursory examination reveals that their lives are riddled with pain and heartache.

It would appear that a good deal of this pain has been caused by disillusionment with men. Hallie's hatred of men, already focused in her description of men as a "pack of lice" is fortified later in her statements that men "took every cent she [Lily] had, and then spat in her face. Well, maybe I'm teaching her a little bit of sense now" (p. 281). The source of her lesbianism seems at least in this case rooted to manifestly negative experiences and negative attitudes toward men. Hallie, or "Hank" as Mrs. Murdock sardonically calls her later, emerges in the rather undisguised emulation of the aggressive male role.[127]

Indeed, Hallie's shocking remark to Lily, "Do you want me to do what I had to do the last time? . . . Do you want me to strike you, in front of Tiny One, here?" (p. 286), is raw and brutal testimony to the sadistic element in their relationship.

Lily Wynton's alliance with Hallie, on the other hand, seems also desperately tied to her own bitter and abusive experiences with men. You'll "find out what he's really like" (p. 284), says Lily to Mrs. Murdock, referring to Mrs. Murdock's husband, as she warns Mrs. Murdock of the pitfalls of marriage. In spite of love, he will bring "fancy women into the house," and as for her own sad forays with wedded bliss, Lily can only bitterly recall that her husband ultimately deceived her, humiliated her, and ended up with all her money. "That's all they want, marry them or not. They say it's love, but it isn't" (. 288).

As for Mrs. Murdock, her search for romance in life, which sent her brimming with hope to Hallie Noyes and Lily Wynton, sends her quickly in the last sequence back to the loving arms of her husband, a safe harbor, more serene and romantic, she is certain, than the polluted seas into which she has ventured. But "Darling Jim" proves to be the final and most terrible disillusionment. The planned and secret party to celebrate her return to contentment with Jim, which would make her willing" renunciation of all the glory of the world" is brought to a murderous halt before she has crossed the threshold. "'Oh hello,' he said to her. He looked at his paper, and kept his eyes there. 'What did you do? Did you drop up to Hank Noyes's?'" (p. 289). The remark has its desired effect. His planned, almost methodical determination to destroy the potential of Mrs. Murdock's adventure succeeds. Her dreams to escape from the hum-drum conventionalities of married life by either experience or illusion are ended by his bitter words.

It is instructive to examine Mr. Murdock's last series of calculated remarks as indicative of his intentions to dominate, and hence silence his partner.

Jim first refers caustically to Hallie as "Hank or Bill" (p. 289) then intentionally jokes about "what's-her-name, . . . the movie star" (p. 290). He draws more pain with the mock suggestion that little Mrs. Murdock will no doubt be "going on the stage now" (p. 290). Despite Mrs. Murdock's protestation that the experience was something of importance to her that she would remember all her life, Jim is relentless in his derision and reaches deep into his repertoire of abrasive verbal cruelty by suggesting with cutting sarcasm that Miss Wynton's most glorified accomplishment of the afternoon was probably that she could "hang by her feet" (p. 290). Destroyed by the onslaught of his commentary, Mrs. Murdock, who had hoped to recapture a moment of lost romance, is reduced to silent, weary resignation and the monotonous, lonely return to her bedroom. The image of her diminutivization at the hands of her self-righteous husband denies her any actual dimension in her household. The only status open to her is perpetual childhood. She embodies no legitimate reality to her husband. Mrs. Murdock has no choice but to live under and accept the reality imposed by her husband, or in the "patriarchal order male reality has usually been posited as the only reality."[128] In this sense, Mr. Murdock, the dominant male figure is actually limited to his own definitions of reality, while Mrs. Murdock as the muted female figure not only understands his definitions—but understands more besides.[129]

By silencing his wife, Mr. Murdock chooses to be a victim of his own limitations. Her statement, "All right, Jim . . . If that's the way you want to be" (p. 290) complies in a silence that should not be construed as either agreement or lack of additional or contrary information. Indeed, throughout the story Mrs. Murdock is perpetually treated like a child by both men and women. Hallie's diminutive nickname, "Tiny One," coupled with Lily Wynton's persistent direct reference to Mrs. Murdock as "little Clever-Face" (p. 285) and her commands as she blacked out to "go, child" (p. 288) preclude Mrs. Murdock from achieving any sense of immanence from either the dominant males or the aggressive females in the story.

However, the loss of Mrs. Murdock's girlish illusion as a result of her experience with either the lesbian Miss Noyes or the actress Mrs. Wynton are relatively minor compared to the emotional awakening to her true relationship with her husband. It is thus no surprise in the final scene, that "Wearily she left the room" (p. 290) and "Wearily little Mrs. Murdock went on down the hall to her bedroom" (p. 290), drained of emotion but not before she stopped at the pantry to ask the maid to put the things she had bought for Jim "somewhere." Her next sentence, "I thought we might have them some time" (p. 290) marks the experience with a verbal statement of defeat and resignation. The first words, "I thought," represent a perception hedged in doubt and hesitation. Mrs. Murdock's uncertainty, voiced in a traditional female lexicon, allows her only to "think," i.e., speculate, rather than to know. The relationship between the personal pronoun "I" and "we" indicates that the "I" has no real power to determine for the "we." The language used is conditional; hence what was thought as possible by the "I" pronoun is conditioned by the use of the contingency verb "might" for the "we" pronoun. Her intentions are negated by the non-committal word "might," which indicates concession, and her language is restrained and invaded by doubt. Consider the difference between:

> I thought we might have them some time" (p. 290) and
> We will have them later.

The speaker relinquishes her authority and in deferential learned politeness agrees to uncertainty even to herself through a syntactic device.

The adverbial construction "some time" suggests an indefinite abstract answer to the critical question, When? The exotic delicacies of "red caviar" (p. 289) and esoteric "foreign cheese" (p. 289), the props that Parker furnished to Mrs. Murdock as romantic symbols, are apathetically handed to the maid to be vaguely put "somewhere" for "some time." So doing, Mrs. Murdock consigns herself to a life without enchantment.

What happens in this story is that the author shares with the reader insights about the poignant tragedies of all three women. Far from a surface parody of a lesbian, an actress, and a housewife, the story illuminates a view of women who, though they each seek romance and escape from the commonness of life in distinctly different ways, are drawn ineluctably into disillusionment and lovelessness. Hallie Noyes's attempts at bohemianism are as artless and shallow as the plasticine torsos of Eve she models. Her lesbian relationship with Lily Wynton is an empty, frightening arrangement with dark hints of sadism and intimidation. Hallie openly strikes Lily for over-indulgence, punishes her for drinking, and verbally threatens her for misbehaving. Lily conversely, begs her erstwhile female lover for pitiful favors and permissions, "Please, sweet Hallie, . . . pretty please. Poor, poor Lily" (p. 286). Hallie Noyes's cheap, flirtatious gestures toward Mrs. Murdock as she "lightly kissed her mouth" (p. 282) and patted "Mrs. Murdock's knee as she passed her" (p. 287) are testimony to the transitory and evanescent nature of her lesbian relationship with Lily.

Lily Wynton, on the other hand, is a mass of alcoholism, acidity, and physical decay. Parasitic and decrepit, Lily pendulates between a variety of sufferings that have taken their toll over the years. Hallie, as Lily's nursemaid and keeper, is as trapped by Lily's maladies and excesses as Lily is trapped by Hallie's intimidation and aggressiveness. There is little glamour, love, or beauty in their sad relationship. Lily clings to the vestiges of her former greatness, but her remembrances of Shakespeare's great lines recounting the seven ages of man, trail off conspicuously, with "the infant, mewling and puking—" (p.286), a reverberation of her present life. Her hopes of love and romance dashed by the vicissitudes of excessiveness and immoderate living, she herself lost to the clutches of a loveless relationship with a dominant lesbian, she aptly laments the death of romance in her life as she closes her famous eyes and rhapsodizes "To sleep, perchance to dream" (p. 287).

Ironically, Mrs. Murdock's dream of romance was a "brave, beautiful men living and dying for the lady who was the pale bride of art, whose eyes and heart were soft with only compassion for them" (p. 281). Yet, conspicuously absent in this story about romantic female desire is the presence, even the hint, of any "brave beautiful men," and as Lily Wynton inserted her "gloved finger in the corner of her mouth, and dragged it to the side" complaining of toothaches and muttering "Oogh! . . . Oogh!" (p. 287), the "pale bride of art" (p. 281) was surely sentenced to metaphoric death.

Prior to her departure for home, Mrs. Murdock utters on five separate occasions, statements which begin, "I'm afraid." Taken in sequence they are:

> "I'm afraid," little Mrs. Murdock began. (p. 287)
>
> "I'm afraid" she said, "I really must be going home." (p. 287)
>
> "I'm afraid I didn't realize how awfully late it was." (p. 288)
>
> "I'm afraid—I'm afraid I didn't quite understand," Mrs. Murdock said. (p. 288)
>
> I—I'm afraid it is really terribly late." (p. 288)

In this repeated linguistic design of feminine politeness, Mrs. Murdock's etiquette expresses more than a female pattern of good manners. The language conceals in linguistic verbiage the real fear and confusion of her immediate experience and the awakening that awaits her as well. She is "afraid" to some extent of the realities of a life without illusions, and she does not fully "understand" the realities of either her transient adventure or her intransigent marriage.

Parker creates a verbal merging between the fears and confusion of her abstract inner world and the concrete language of her external physical world. Hence, she is indeed "afraid" and does not "understand."

Tentative, naive and love-starved, Mrs. Murdock repeatedly seeks escape in lush fantasies and romantic fictions. Indeed, as she rushes homeward, significantly "through the clustering dark" gathering about her, her mind rationalizes affectionately and innocently that Jim, whom she knows to be "still and cross and silent," is really "Funny Jim, still and cross and silent, but only because he knew so much. Only because he knew the silliness of seeking afar for the glamour and beauty and romance of living" (p. 289), which were right at home after all. The true drama of discovery still awaits her.

Freed of the eccentricities of the two women, Mrs. Murdock's momentary sense of relief and well-being with her own sweet life is abruptly ended by her husband's abrasiveness and insensitivity. Ambivalent, but euphoric over her tea-time adventure, she is aware that the event has special meaning to her—though she has not yet assimilated its significance. Mr. Murdock, on the other hand, may realistically understand more about the actual relationship between Hallie and Lily, but his lack of kindness and his cross words serve only to darken the light in Mrs. Murdock's eyes and simultaneously extinguish the glow of romance she seeks to kindle in his heart.

The author has invited the reader to witness in the end the death of romance. The study reflects finally the sordidness, boredom, and banality that permeates the lives of all three women who pursue without success the romance of living.

Although early in her marriage to Alan, Parker herself evidenced genuine signs of radiant and romantic love, it was short lived. It was not long after their arrival in Hollywood that she began telling humiliating stories about him, frequently in his presence. She was responsible for often placing him in a false light, not only fabricating incidents of his abuse to her, but also spreading the belief that suspicions of his sexual ambivalence were true.

Friends, who felt Alan was wonderful for her, believed she had no right to be so cruel. Adding to her discontent was the fact that while Campbell found Hollywood congenial, Parker was often homesick and lonely, and reacted by initiating terrible arguments with him. Nonetheless, the stark psychological pattern appeared repeatedly in her life; fundamentally, Parker resented and often punished anyone who loved her or tried to help her. As in the case of the women she wrote about and ridiculed, Parker personally found little success in the "romance of living."

Unlikely Heroine: "The Lovely Leave" (1943)

When the United States entered World War II, many Hollywood writers, directors, and actors volunteered to produce training films for the United States Army. However, at the age of forty, surprisingly encouraged by Dorothy, Alan Campbell enlisted in the Army and left Dorothy, who had been turned down by the WACS because of her age, (she was past fifty), envious, proud and resentful at being a war-wife. Parker knew how difficult it was for a man to be both a husband and a soldier. Twenty-five years earlier, she had seen a young husband (Edwin Parker) go off to war to return a stranger.

As soon as Alan was commissioned as a Lieutenant in the Air Force, Dorothy began exhibiting disturbing ambivalent behavior toward him. She was subject to unbearable fits of fury. She became moody, irrational, and paranoid. She could not accept any kind of existence that separated them. She asked Alan why he couldn't wait to be drafted. She accused him of deserting her by enlisting. She quarrelled with him up to the moment he left, but as soon as he was gone, she desperately longed for him, cried in the nights over the mess she had made, and suffered with excruciating guilt.

The splintering effects on their relationship were predictable. Every furlough ended up in disaster despite Dorothy's passionate resolve to make things perfect. Proud and jealous of his handsome youthful looks in uniform, Parker cursed him when they were apart, cursed him when they were together, and cursed him in strange and senseless letters planted with obscene vulgarities that came with directions for decoding.

Alan, on the other hand, had gained a whole new life. While he loved his new friends, the camaraderie of the air-corps, and the exhilaration of military life in general, Dorothy seemed disgusted by it, and sensed that he was often relieved to be free of her. When he left for Europe in November, 1943, Parker returned to New York feeling lonely and purposeless, but managed to produce from the remnants of her heartache, one of her finest pieces, "The Lovely Leave."[130]

While "The Lovely Leave" is fiction and the Lieutenant and his wife are not literally Lieutenant and Mrs. Campbell, the story revealed much about the relationship between Alan and Dorothy. Their styles of speech, the awkwardness and self-consciousness between them when Alan enlisted, the strangeness of Alan in uniform, his concern for his comrades, as well as the explosive emotional exchanges, parallel their mutual experience under the same conditions. The war ultimately extracted a terrible price from them both.

"The Lovely Leave" concerns a young woman's disappointment when her soldier husband's leave from the service is unexpectedly shortened. Mimi McVicker, like many women in New York City in 1943, found life away from Steve dull and tedious. When he called unexpectedly to tell her of the leave next week, she was ecstatic. "There would be no waste to this leave" (p. 4), she vowed. She had not seen Steve in two months, and his previous leave, the first time she had seen him in his Lieutenant's uniform, strangely ended in a quarrel. As she hung up the phone, she thought of the "preposterous shyness that had fallen upon her" (p. 4) when he had come home before and the awkward nervousness over his departure. She silently determined that this twenty-four-hour leave would be redeemed in perfect union.

During the week, Mimi carefully prepared for Steve's arrival. She bought a new black dress ("he liked black dresses," p. 6), a delightful chiffon nightgown, his favorite salted biscuits, and six pots of potted fuchsia with "delicate parchment-colored inverted cups and their graceful magenta bells" (p. 7). Even if she went without lunches the next week because of her extravagance, it would be all right.

When Steve arrives, he brings the shattering news that his leave is cut short. "We're to go right on to the new field. I've got to get a train at six-ten," (p. 9) he announces. With less than an hour left to them, the McVickers face the anxiety of perfecting the impossibly short time they have together. Under the strain of Mini's disappointment, they quarrel and Mimi disclosed her buried resentment over Steve's devotion to the service. "You see," she said with care, "You have a whole new life—I have half an old one. Your life is so far away from mine. I don't see how they're even going to come back together" (p. 11).

In an effort to avoid confrontation over a subject that makes him uneasy and in order to savor, for a few moments the comforts of home, Steve decides to take a bath, leisurely read a magazine, and spend his last minutes polishing his pilot's belt buckle, much to Mimi's disappointment.

At the time of his departure, Steve speaks with difficulty about his feelings, telling Mimi he "belongs" (p. 17) with her despite his job. She rushes to his open arms as he leaves, and when a friend calls moments later to inquire about the leave, she responds to her sympathy over its cancellation by saying, "I know it wasn't very much time. But oh, it was lovely" (p. 18).

"The Lovely Leave" addresses the different ways women and men handle affection and emotion. One of Parker's concerns in the story is the verbal resources permitted to a woman for the candid expression of feeling, both physical and emotional. As we seek to formulate the view of women that emerges in this work, a number of questions come to mind. Are the emotions the primary province of women? Are women's emotions viewed differently from men in time of crisis? Are the loneliness and struggle of a woman less important that the same experiences in a man? Are there rules for emotional intercourse that must be obeyed only by one gender and not by the other? If so, who decides on these rules? In what ways can a man shut out from his world a woman he loves?

The story is set against a war-time environment in 1943. Mimi McVicker's emotional response to her husband's absence because of the war seems initially possessive and self-serving.

Our first apprehension of Mimi McVicker's private sensibilities is revealed rather unexpectedly in the opening scene. As she cradles the telephone that has just brought the news of her husband's impending leave, she looks at it "as if all frustration and bewilderments and separations were at its fault." The telephone now enshrined with new symbolic importance, had brought her his longed-for voice, but it was a voice she noted that was "brisk and busy," and the gay, wild, young voices coming from the background, familiar to him and not to her, were the "voices of those who shared his new life" (p. 3). When she begs him for an extra minute to speak, Steven heeds the clamoring voices in th background not hers. The details of the next passage are worth noting:

> She took her hand off the telephone and held it away from her with the fingers spread stiffly apart, as if she had touched something horrid. (p. 3)

The touch of the telephone evokes powerful feelings of horror. Mimi clearly attached deeper meaning to Steve's abruptness over the phone and his return to the young men who need him.

A close review of Mimi's immediate thoughts provides the reader with a number of explanations.

> If you look for things to make you feel hurt and wretched and unnecessary, you were certain to find them, more easily each time, so easily soon, that you did not even realize you had gone out searching. Women alone often developed into experts at the practice. She must never join their dismal league. (p. 4)

It is clear that Mimi already harbors feelings of "hurt" and "wretchedness" and that she suspects for some reason that she is unnecessary." The disaster of Steve's first leave was the result of her "gangling diffidence" with this stranger in uniform combined with the golden time she spoiled in "grudging its going" (p. 4). Their quarrel in the last hours as Steve became "nervous under the pall" provided a cool and formal good-bye, "no clinging farewells" (p. 4), which left Mimi "striking her breast and sobbing" (p. 5). In the months following his last leave she pondered what had happened, and she concluded privately that she had wrought an "ugly small ruin" (p. 5). There is already suggestive inference in the language of Mimi's ruminations that draws together the phrases "unnecessary," "gangling diffidence," "no clinging farewells" and an "ugly small ruin" as a reflection of Mimi's half-conscious appraisal of the discordant sexual harmony of her marriage. Do these concerns somehow link with the voices of the gay young men in the background and the feeling of horror from the touch of the phone? It is already clear that Steven's "new life" (p. 11) as an army officer carries an unspoken threat to her marriage.

After all, it was true that this had been the first time the young married couple had been separated. The disaster of their first reunion must not be repeated. Hence, Mimi's instant resolve to create tenderness and excitement and a whole long day of shining sweet love for Steve seized her imagination. This leave would be the crucible for their love. Perhaps, she thought deeply, that the "strange new life" and " strange gay voices" would have no existence for "two who were really one" (p. 6). What nagging perilous meaning does Mimi attach to these thoughts of "strange new life" and "gay voices" that go beyond her recognition of Steve's conventional devotion to his duty?

With ebullient attention to every detail, Mimi thrusts herself into the preparations for Steve's homecoming. She will create an alluring and provocative atmosphere in which seductively she can win back her warrior. The expensive black dress, the chiffon nightgown "with innocent puffs of sleeves," the costly materials for cocktails and whiskies-and-sodas, the potted fuchsias, the perfume and toilet water and bath oil comprise her female arsenal. It is particularly interesting, even amusing, that on the day of Steve's arrival Mimi sings as she dresses in the bedroom a lusty masculine song that sounds somewhat "ludicrous" (p. 7) in her hesitant little voice:

> "Here they come: zooming to meet our thunder—
> At 'em boys, give 'er the gun!" (p. 8)

As she savors the last line of her melody, it seems clear that Mimi's preoccupations, both conscious and unconscious, revolve around claiming a sexual victory with Steve and reawakening his physical love for her.

Steve's arrival finds them in each other's arms, as "she slid her cheek along his lips, touched her forehead to his shoulder, and broke away" (p. 9). We note this inconspicuous detail that "she slid her cheek along his lips" rather than pressing her lips to his, followed by the more deliberate act of breaking away.

Her next line, the greeting "Nice to see you, Lieutenant. How's the war?" extends the feelings of self-consciousness and awkwardness we sense in their embrace and puts their relationship on a formal plane. He is the "lieutenant" and this is a "war." The uniform has done it again, and the intimacy she has hoped for is already strained.

His appearance without "a bag," as Mimi observes nervously, coupled with his immediate announcement that the leave is cancelled, visibly strain Mimi's already taut emotions, as his common-sense response to the inevitable is set against the passionate cravings of her heart and body. Furthermore, it appears that Steve's controlled attitude and actions may signal more than heroic military devotion and may indeed serve a personal desire.

From the time he arrives, it seems evident that Steve wishes to avoid intimate physical and emotional contact with his wife. Whatever claims his "strange new life" (p. 6) have laid upon him, they are sufficient now to insinuate themselves profoundly between them.

Arriving without a bag, spouting platitudes, like "This is the Army, Mrs. Jones" and "There's War On" (p. 10), Steve retreats into an unsentimental and impersonal relationship with Mimi, which serves to engorge her brimming anger and exacerbate her growing resentments toward her husband's seeming withdrawal from her life. Steve's constant references to the hardships of the military and his admiration for the boys provoke Mimi to comment that she doesn't give "a damn about the boys" (p. 10), which in turn drives Steve to blurt out, "Are you—are you jealous of the pilots?" (p. 11).

It was well known that Parker had long built the legend of Alan's persistent homosexuality as part of the cargo of her marriage, apparently with little outright verification, but as a punitive act of dominance. Hence, the references in the story to "jealousy of the pilots," "gay voices," and "new life" among the men are easily transfigured into Dorothy's real life fears about Alan's sexual preferences. "I can compete with the girls, but not the boys,"[131] she disdainfully remarked to Charles Addams. Simultaneously, Dorothy also worried about his infidelity with women. When Alan was stationed in London with Air Force Intelligence, the tone of his letters were brimming with undisguised excitement. He was having a lovely time.

There were suggestions about gracious dinner parties, attractive society women, cryptic weekends, and historic palatial country houses. Dorothy began to suspect that Alan was having an affair with a woman. In 1944 she published the poem, "War Song," dedicated to Lieutenant Campbell, sympathetically portraying an American soldier making love to a foreign girl as part of the expectations of wartime romance. In what appeared, at least in print, as an astonishingly liberated view, Dorothy exempted Alan, indeed all American soldiers from a commitment to celibacy. In addition, she virtually gave her husband permission to sleep with anyone he liked, indeed encouraging him not to feel guilty. Her one caveat was stated in the final line:

> War Song
> Soldier, in a curious land
> 　All across a swaying sea,
> Take her smile and lift her hand—
> 　Have no guilt of me.
> Soldier, when were soldiers true?
> 　If she's kind and sweet and gay,
> Use the wish I send to you—
> 　Lie not lone till day!
> Only, for the nights that were,
> 　Soldier, and the dawns that came,
> When in sleep you turn to her
> 　Call her by my name.

Misunderstood and vilified for lack of proper womanly attitude, Parker was viciously criticized by an outraged public who could accept her views as facts of life.

However, Mimi McVicker, the protagonist of the story, (which pre-dates the poem by one year,) is not prepared to embrace Parker's polemic if indeed Parker's extraordinary tolerance is to be taken seriously. Mimi is plainly jealous.

It is instructive to contemplate at this point precisely how and why Mimi's womanly loneliness and love have been transmogrified into her present resentment and jealously. Part of the answer is to be found by examining the division within Mimi as a passionate and emotional woman in conflict with a dutiful and obedient wife. This duality finds a correlative for women in the delicate balance between what is forbidden and what can be said.[132]

As a war wife, Mimi McVicker struggles to be heroic and dutiful toward her soldier husband. She knows, for example,

> There had been rules to be learned in that matter, and the first of them was the hardest: never say to him what you want him to say to you. ..Do not bedevil him with the pinings of your faithful heart because he is your husband, your man, your love. For you are writing to none of these. You are writing to a soldier. (p. 6)

Mimi understood the rules, hence she had never sent him a letter of complaint or sadness or anger. She surmised if her letters were careful and chosen, then, as a reward, when they were together "there would be no stiltedness" (p. 6). Mimi has already surrendered to the notion of a male-imposed definition regarding what is appropriate behavior as a wife[133] and even prays, "Please keep me from doing wrong things. Please let it be lovely" (p. 8). She tries unsuccessfully through spirited gallantry ("Nice to see you, Lieutenant. How's the war? p. 9) to disguise her loneliness. But her dark fears and mounting jealousy when she finally tries to express these feelings are dismissed as inappropriate nonsense by her irritated husband who has more important things on his mind.

She tries, carefully, to give him a "glimpse" (p. 12) of her heart, but her candor is punished: "You see," Steve complains, "I don't know what to say, when you start talking about showing me glimpses of your heart, and all that" (p. 13).

We see that they love each other, but as they reach toward one another, invariably one of them does or says some selfish thing that triggers anger in the other. The awareness of the time swiftly passing as well as their own awkwardness and self-consciousness conspire against them as each fails to understand the other at the exact moment when it is crucial to do so. For example, when Steve tries belatedly to compliment her new black dress, she snaps "I almost wish I were in it for another reason." When he suggests that she is "silly" not to go out with some of their male friends, she snarls, "It hadn't occurred to me. . .that it was silly to be faithful to one's husband" (p. 12). This line strikes us in sharp contrast to Parker's position in "War Song" and certainly admits to a surprising double standard for men and women.

They feel and talk at cross-purposes, at odds in both language and behavior. She longs for compliments and little gestures of affection, while Steve savors the pleasures of a comfortable chair, a new magazine, and a hot bath. "You have a whole new life," she concludes, "I have half an old one. . .I don't see how they're even going to come back together" (p. 11).

Mimi's resentments not only focus on Steve's new life as an officer who seems to love his work and his men too much, but there are also hints of his apathy and neglect toward their marriage since he has been in the service. Mimi makes subtle, caustic references to his lack of mail to her, is hurt by his suggestion that she might want to go out to dinner with some male friends, since "It's possible to go out with a man and stay this side of adultery" (p. 12)—a bitter reward for one's faithfulness, she argues—and is offended by his comment that she must be having a rotten time, but is probably just "feeling fairly sorry" (p. 13) for herself.

Until now, Steve's physical attention to Mimi has been less than excessive, though she has sought to make loving gestures to him by sitting on the arm of his chair and burying her face in his shoulder. Her attempts are met by Steve's comment: "This is more like it" (p. 10), which Mimi learns to her disappointment refers to the comfort of the chair rather than her caresses.

Only at one point does Steve burst spontaneously into apparent amorous passion. The moment provides the reader with some interesting speculation. In response to Steve's comment that he'd like to think of Mimi as "having a good time" while he was away, Mimi kisses him on the forehead, remarking" 'You are a far nobler character than I am. Either that,' she said, 'or there is something else in back of this.'" Steve's joking response: "Oh, shut up" is spoken as "he pulled her down to him and held her there." But even as her body seemed "to melt against him," she noticed that "he was craning over her shoulder endeavoring to see his wrist watch" (p. 13).

What is the reader to make to these obvious incongruities in Steve's responses to his wife? In the first place, we note that Steve's ardor seems triggered by Mimi's suggestion that either he is "noble" in his desires for his wife to have a "good time" while he is away, or there is something else in back of this. It is the "something else" that provokes Steve's jesting verbal response "Oh, shut up," which perhaps should not be regarded so lightly, and galvanizes his short lived passion. Has Mimi unknowingly come too close to something that Steve prefers to divert by his sudden expression of lust? His protestations that "we've—we've only a little while darling," seem specious, and his sudden desire to "take a bath" as he advised Mimi to "get up" (p. 13) are dense with connotative inferences regarding the cause of his sexual disinterest in his wife.

Both physically and verbally Mimi has been denied fulfillment of expression. Her own vindictive comment to Steve as he enters the bath, "I suppose they [the boys] can't bear being parted from you" (p. 15) causes her to think of the "nightgown with the little bouquets" lying untouched in the bureau. The jealous anger toward the men and the unconscious sexual tie between the "boys" and the "nightgown" provoke speculation as to Mimi's unspoken anxiety about Steve's attachments and invite further suspicion in the reader's mind over the cause of Steve's lack of sexual interest in his wife. In desperation Mimi is driven to expression that is wholly nonverbal. "She went over to the bathroom door, drew back her right foot, and kicked the base of the door so savagely that the whole frame shook." Ironically, Steve's question "Want something?" is returned by Mimi's bitter piece of sarcasm, "Nothing whatever. I've got everything any woman could possibly want, haven't I?" (p. 15).

Clearly at work here is the difference in emotional architecture between a richly passionate woman who seeks expression and intimacy with a man and a detached preoccupied soldier who prefers distance and the camaraderie of military life with the boys. What is not clear and has apparently been overlooked by the few critical commentaries available is the possibility that Steve's ardent and growing attachment to his men already preclude him from physically desiring his wife's love and stir in him a deeper longing as a man. The central romance of his life has become the war and his boys. "You don't care about anything but those pilots" (p. 10), Mimi argues, unaware that her words may carry more profound meaning that her intentions. On another level, Parker's uneasiness about Alan's homosexuality are ratified in those lines.

Relegated to an acquiescent role of silence and support, forbidden free fulfillment of her feelings as though they were a betrayal of the war effort, Mimi, whose first name may be an ironic reproach for her self-absorption, has become an outsider. "The Lieutenant," as she repeatedly refers to him, is indeed a "stranger," and the "preposterous shyness" (p. 4) that came upon her when she first saw him in uniform and returned to her as he appeared that day was symptomatic of the alienation from his life that was subversively taking place.

This alienation takes many subtle forms. Steve's army language, satirized by Parker as a form of "men's language," effectively excludes Mimi from his most basic reference points, as in this exchange between the soldier husband and his wife when he searches for a cloth in order to polish his belt buckle:

> "Hell, I don't suppose you've got a Blitz Cloth, have you? Or a Shine-O?"
>
> "If I had the faintest idea what you were talking about," she said, "I might be better company for you." (p. 5)

By selecting vocabulary from an exclusively male orientation, Steve maintains his dominance over Mimi, encourages her sense of awkwardness in his presence, and denies her access to equal participation in their relationship.[134]

Steve's sexual rejection furthermore carries the potent threat of death to Mimi as a woman. Defined primarily in her society in terms of sexuality, Mimi is obsessed less by her sexual desire, and more by her sexual desirability, a standard created by men and accepted by women. Her power to attract men is the life-giving measure of her womanhood. When she feels the loss of this power, she simultaneously feels the life force draining from her.[135]

Mimi's long speech to her husband probes her deep emotional confusion over their relationship and touches on the effect the war has had on her as a woman. In some of Parker's most mature and straightforward language, Mimi pleads for herself and makes a case for any woman who has felt alienation and rejection by men whose absorption in male-identified causes has trivialized their importance.

I'm trying to tell you something. Just because you've got on that pretty suit, you think you should never hear anything serious, never anything sad or wretched or disagreeable. You make me sick, that's what you do? . . . I realize what you're doing, I told you what I think of it. Don't for heaven's sake, think I'm mean enough to grudge you any happiness and excitement you can get out of it. I know it's hard for you. But it's never lonely, that's all I mean. You have companionship no-no wife can ever give you. I suppose it's the sense of hurry, maybe the consciousness of living on borrowed time, the—the knowledge of what you're all going through together that makes the comradeship of men in war so firm, so fast. But won't you please try to understand how I feel? Won't you understand that it comes out of bewilderment and disruption and—and being frightened, I guess? Won't you understand what makes me do what I do, when I hate myself while I'm doing it?[136] (pp. 16-17)

The speech is the heart of the story. A moving and impassioned plea, it is the rhetoric of an intelligent, feeling woman who demands to be heard on a matter that has been declared off-limits to her. Though she risks a great deal, Mimi raises a number of serious women's issues that she can no longer avoid. In the first place, she attacks Steve's chauvinistic attitude, that endows him with automatic immunity from Mimi's feelings as long as he is in uniform and ensures that an honest relationship between a woman and her soldier is nearly impossible during wartime. The fact that the rules call for nothing "wretched" or "disagreeable" to be said to an army man finally makes Mimi "sick." She knows that women have an easier time in the war, but she also knows that men seem to derive a peculiar "excitement" from army life, which she senses, and wisely, does not begrudge. But it is on the issue of "companionship" and "comradeship" that she takes her strongest stand. The allusion to the press of time, the urgency and importance of what they are going through, and the threat of death that hovers about them are sufficient reasons to draw men together in a bond of companionship that cannot be challenged—not even by a wife.

Yet, admittedly this is the source of her jealousy, her fear, and her resentment: jealousy of the life and love he has with his men while she is lonely, fear that she has lost him to it in more ways than she can explain, and resentment that he has rejected her from his new life, disrupted her old one, and cast her away from him as an emotional outsider, an hysterical female who has no place in or understanding of a man's war. It is a brave speech. It is patently female and is one of the clearest and truest pictures of uncluttered womanly emotions in Parker's repertoire.

Mimi's painful mixture of anger and longing are part of the casualties of a war that will exact a price from both of them. Her jealousy of his comrades, the "bewilderment and disruption" (p.17), her fear of loneliness and estrangement mingle and erupt in her as a protest primarily against her life as a female outsider.

One also cannot ignore her blunt insistence that "you have companionship no—no wife can ever give you" (p. 17). What she knows or fears about that companionship is not pursued.

In 1944, as Parker awaited her husband's return from London, she wrote a passionate article called "Who Is That Man?" based upon these same apprehensions of "strangeness" and alienation that Mimi McVickers had solemnly expressed toward her soldier-husband.

> "Who is this man, who will come back to you? You know him as he was,. . .But what will he be, this stranger who comes back? How are you to throw a bridge cross the gap that has separated you. . .what have you to offer him? There are pictures in his memory that he can never share with you. . .Make a friend out of that stranger from across the world."[137]

We can appreciate the strain on Parker somehow to achieve perspective. We sense the full pattern of her fears as she acknowledges the incompatibility of men and women who have been divided and estranged by war. Parker failed, however, to follow her own admonitions. Her relationship with Campbell, which was severely damaged by their separation, was prophesied in Mimi McVicker's words, rather than her own.

The image of Mimi's life as fragmented, disoriented, inferiorized, and purposeless is not lost upon the reader. But how fully Steve understands her invocation is another matter. His eyes misted and troubled, he is able to bring himself with difficulty to say: "I can't talk about it. I can't even think about it—because if I did I couldn't do my job. . . I want to be with you, Mimi. That's where I belong (p. 11). While his words seem genuine and touching enough, marked by the proper, fairly perfect balance between emotion and duty, we are left to decipher the meaning of his actions. As he holds his arms open to Mimi, she runs to them and in an embrace seemingly unlike their greeting earlier when she "slid her cheek along his lips" (p. 9), the author tells us, "This time, she did not slide her cheek along his lips" (p. 18). With the next sentence, Steve is gone.

While we are told that, "This time she [Mimi] did not slide her cheeks along his lips," hinting that she meets Steve more passionately, the description is sufficiently ambivalent and Steve's exit unexpectedly abrupt. The author leaves the reader room to speculate. Though it appears that their parting is marked by some mutual exchange of real emotion (if we read passion into her final gesture), the reader is struck by the fact that even to the end, it is Mimi who runs to Steve with the offer of love, as he stands rooted to the spot his arms extended in a dutiful and mannered gesture of invitation.

When he is gone, Mimi turns her attention and the reader's interest, to the fuchsia plants, an image recurring with regularity throughout the story. Earlier, brimming with excitement and romantic optimism over Steve's arrival, Mimi could not resist the charming flowers with their "delicate parchment-colored inverted cups and their graceful magenta bells" (p. 7). Later, as she stood outside the bathroom breathing heavily with anger scarring her palms with her fingernails over Steve's intolerable indifference, she looked at the fuchsia blossoms "with their dirty parchment-colored caps, their vulgar magenta bells" (p. 15). Finally, after her farewell embrace with Steve, she returns her gaze to the fuchsia plants, "touching delicately, tenderly, the enchanting parchment-colored caps, the exquisite magenta bells" (p. 18). Clearly the aesthetic transformations of the plants in the eye of the beholder are metaphoric parallels to Mimi's inner emotional state, as they change from "delicate" and "graceful," to "dirty" and "vulgar," to "enchanting" and "exquisite." Does this transformation at the end lead us to conclude that the final image of the "enchanting parchment-colored caps, the exquisite magenta bells," bodes a happy ending for Mimi? Probably not. It is true that in the end Mimi and Steve did cling to each other in a farewell marked by confused emotions. Compared to the cool and silent goodbye after Steve's first leave, when he cleared his throat and said," Guess, I'd better get going" (p. 5) as Mimi stood watching him in the middle of the floor, this final farewell gives legitimate cause for some degree of happiness. However, do they actually find each other at the instant of their parting? Or is it too late? Too little time?

It appears that the lingering effects of Mimi's momentary and confused rapture are brought to a sudden end by the harsh sound of the telephone. As we listen carefully to Mimi's response to her friend's offer of sympathy, that it was a shame, "absolutely terrible" (p. 18) that all leaves were cancelled, we cannot resist the conclusion that Mimi's words are neither true in fact nor honest in emotion. "I know it wasn't very much time but oh, it was lovely!" (p. 18). The hollowness of the words fall heavily on our ears, as Mimi once again in her solitude is forced not only to an appraisal of the past, but to an estimate of the future. Her womanly guile, which conditioned her earlier to learn the "rules" (p. 6), to protect and conceal, to deny her own urges, empowers her now with the ability to gloss over the truth and parget her experience into a particularly female expression of conciliation, as she says quite deceptively: "But oh, it was lovely." The story is Parker's unusually straightforward effort to explore in writing the conflict of Mimi's private battles as a woman sharing a man's war.

For Parker, the war story had a different ending. When in 1945, at the end of the war, Alan remained overseas in London, just as Edwin Parker had remained in the occupation forces in 1918, Dorothy distraught and enraged, spread the word that the reason for Alan's extended stay in London was a homosexual affair—not military duty.

In reality, Alan had fallen in love with a married woman who was a wealthy and titled aristocrat. The affair was to be kept secret. Dorothy was stunned and responded with her usual patterns during personal crisis; drink, depression, vindictiveness. She consulted a psychiatrist, claimed to be receiving electro-shock treatments, and declared she was having a nervous breakdown. She bore little resemblance to the staunch heroine of her own story, and certainly no allegiance to her poetic platitudes.

During the two years Alan remained in Europe, Parker waged a personal was against him in this country. Ruthlessly, she publicly depicted his shortcomings, which ranged from personal cowardice to fortune hunting. According to her he "couldn't write;. . .he was weak; . . . he was afraid;. . .he couldn't cook; . . . he never understood her; . . . he couldn't hold his liquor; . . . he wasn't a man; . . . he was a queer and pansy."[138] As for his heralded war record, she claimed he was over their playing "hostess." Unable to follow her own advice, she threw no "bridges across the gaps," and offered no "friendship."

Many friends believed the English romance was Alan's just punishment for Dorothy's abusiveness during the stormy periods of their marriage. Nevertheless, by late 1946, the affair seemed to be on the wane. Alan wrote Dorothy that he was coming home and expected to be reconciled. Dorothy however, could not forgive him and refused to take him back. She informed Campbell that she intended to divorce him.

When he returned to New York, Alan insisted he did not want a divorce. He blamed the war for destroying their marriage, and told reporters, "We had a wonderful time. I'm sorry it's over."[139] Alan claimed he still cared for Dorothy throughout the divorce hearing, and despite unpleasant notoriety, Dorothy's furor subsided and they established amicable relations during and after the dismantling of their marriage. Neither of them could know at that time, that this would not be the end of their relationship.

As for Parker, ironically, "War Song" would be the last poem she would ever publish.

Anatomy of a Divorce: "The Banquet of Crow" (1957)

"The Banquet of Crow,"[140] the artful and disturbing story of an incompatible marriage, prolonged estrangement, and failed reconciliation, was written shortly after Dorothy Parker's unexpected reconciliation with Alan Campbell. After their divorce in 1947, they were remarried in 1950, subsequently separated, and reconciled in 1957.

It was a frightening period. The specter of the anti-Communist inquisition invaded Dorothy's personal and professional life. In 1949, Dorothy was blacklisted after Walter Winchell identified her in a note to the FBI as a "mad fanatic of the Commy party line."[141] Many of her friends, including Zero Mostel and Lillian Hellman were called for contempt, denounced, and even sentenced to prison. Parker herself was summoned to testify, and after politely answering prolonged questions about her political activities regarding aid to Spain and the anti-Nazi movement, she finally ferociously invoked the Fifth Amendment, refusing to answer further questions on the grounds of possible self-incrimination. By 1955, after five years of reviewing her activities, the FBI closed its investigation of her stating she was not "dangerous" enough for inclusion in the Security Index.

The period had traumatized the entire Hollywood community. Alan was terrified of being blacklisted and understood the dangers of his association with Parker, although he remained outwardly loyal and supportive as her husband. Nevertheless, there were signs of internal turmoil in their relationship.

During the summer of 1951, after a violent argument, Alan walked out on their marriage, and according to Dorothy sent a van to strip the house of all its belongings. Dorothy rescued only a bed. Disgusted and bitter, she vowed to end their relationship once and for all.

Despite their separation and the ugliness of his departure, Alan remained concerned for Dorothy's welfare. By 1956, during a period of great strain and unhappiness, Dorothy relented and responded to Alan's persistent phone calls. She admitted her loneliness and expressed continued love for him. By 1957 they were seeing each other, and by 1961, lured by the opportunity to work together on a script for Marilyn Monroe, they were re-united in Hollywood in a precarious relationship, that would remain volatile and bizarre to the end.

Parker was sixty-eight. Her years as a political activist who was blacklisted and subpoenaed by the House on Un-American Activities Committee were over. Her play, *Ladies of the Corrider*, the work she claimed to be most proud of, was not a theatrical success, and her writing had practically stopped. Money was short and the reconciliation with Alan was the first note of hope in what had been a long period of bad times for Parker. She and Alan settled into a small, modest life of quarreling, drinking, and tension-filled tolerance of each other that eventually became comfortable and familiar. But the emotional wreckage of separation and divorce had left its scars.

In "The Banquet of Crow" Parker examines the aftermath of an eleven-year marriage that comes apart when the husband, Guy Allen, leaves his wife, Maida. After years of fruitless explanation to his wife, regarding his own unhappiness, Guy Allen walked in one night and announced quite simply: "I don't want to do this any more Maida, I'm through" (p. 42), and then went out the door, never to come back. Bewildered and clinging to the belief that the marriage was after all "eleven years of perfect happiness" (p. 40), Maida moves through a series of friends and acquaintances who do their "practical best to medicine her wounds" (p. 39). Unconsoled by their cavalier promises that Guy will come back, and ultimately deserted by her circle of friends who become bored with her endless saga of blameless desertion, Maida seeks out Dr. Marjorie Langham, psychiatrist, who assures her that Guy is merely "going through the change" (p. 40).

Fortified by therapy and books by women recognized as authorities in the field, Maida is convinced that Guy will soon return once he has a little "suffering on his own hook" (p. 41). When the miracle happens and Guy calls only to arrange to pick up his suitcase at the apartment, Maida promises Dr. Langham that she will not soften. Indeed, "Guy Allen will eat crow" (p. 41).

That evening, when pressed by Maida, Guy attempts a final explanation of his behavior, Maida still does not hear. He states that he is quite happy with their separation, and announces that he is leaving for San Francisco.

After his departure, Maida constructs a unique fantasy. He'll come back sadder but wiser, with unattractive gray hair. And then she will make him eat crow. "She made a little picture of him, gray and shabby and broken down, gnawing at a leg of cold crow, which she saw with all its feathers left on it, black and shining and disgusting" (p. 43). But the power of the fantasy fades, and Maida silently heads for the telephone to call Dr. Langham.

"The Banquet of Crow" was Dorothy Parker's last published short story, and like her first, "Such a Pretty Little Picture," it deals with a marriage that has only the outward appearance of domestic bliss. While Mr. Wheelock remains fixed in the matriarchal bondage of his marriage ironically depicted as "Such a Pretty Little Picture," Guy Allen chooses to breathe life into Wheelock's recurring fantasies of escape and walk away from his misery. Parker's treatment of failed marriage comes full circle.

The story, however, is less concerned with Guy's desertion, than it is with Maida's reactions. In this sense, the story presents a sensitive study of the ways in which a mature woman attempts to adapt to the profound disaster of her married life. Ostensibly, Maida appears to be the classic avatar, the satiric prototype of the boring well-to-do woman whose abandonment is predictable and earned. But we are soon drawn to consider how and if Maida contributes entirely to her own demise in this marriage.

Though Maida's personality is certainly the controlling element in the story, we do not hear from her as a character until well into the narrative. It is not until the third page of the five-page story that Maida herself speaks. However, the reader gathers extensive information about Maida, her marriage, and the world in which she lives through the accretion of various viewpoints.

The story is told primarily in the third-person narrative, with Maida, Dr. Langham, and Guy adding only bits of dialogue to what is otherwise a descriptive design. That is to say, most of the story tells "about" Maida.

Unusual in its structure, the story opens metaphorically with a newsreel-like passage devoted to a panoramic view of the time and place, obviously upper-middle-class New York City during the late 1950s. With rhythmic staccato, punctuated by sharp repetition, the opening sequence hammers away at the vacuousness and apathy of the times, distilling a disturbing image of a period in America when the nation that apparently had the most of everything still had the best of nothing.

> It was a crazy year, a year when things that should have run on schedule went all which ways. It was a year when snow fell thick and lasting in April, and young ladies clad in shorts were photographed for the tabloids sunbathing in Central Park in January. It was a year when, in the greatest prosperity of the richest nation, you could not walk five city blocks without being besought by beggars; when expensively dressed women loud and lurching

in public places were no uncommon sight; when drugstore counters were stacked with tablets to make you tranquil and other tablets to set you leaping. It was a year . . . when husbands who have come home every evening not only at the same hour but at the same minute of the same hour came home one evening more, spoke a few words, and then went out of their doors and did not come in by them again. (p. 39)

If we isolate and examine carefully the collective images of women depicted in this opening sequence in its entirety, they would appear as follows:

"young ladies clad in shorts were photographed for the tabloids sunbathing in Central Park in January."

"aggressively dressed women loud and lurching in public places were no uncommon sight."

"wives whose position was only an inch or two below that of the saints—arbiters of etiquette, venerated hostesses, architects of memorable menus—suddenly caught up a traveling bag and a jewel case and flew off to Mexico with ambiguous young men allied with the arts." (p. 39)

The immediate impression the reader takes away is one of a society of vacuous, loose, purposeless, self-indulgent females fiercely devoted to fulfilling their own shallow needs. On the other hand, the "young ladies clad in shorts," the "aggressively dressed women," and the society "wives" are all also images of women, in their heated response to men, acting foolishly and desperately. Each of them is engaged in a form of activity that trades on their sexuality and uses it in exchange for a relationship with men. The silly young ladies in shorts sitting in the snow apparently were part of the lunacy in which Guy Allen participated by the insane act of leaving his wife. But the characterization of the incongruities of time in the previous passage has further importance to the plot. Indeed, if Guy Allen had left his wife during another period, the author informs us, Maida would have kept the enduring interest of all her friends. But in this year, remarkable for its excesses, so many marriages had split apart that friends were "overly familiar with tales of shipwrecks" (p. 39). It was in this atmosphere of listless interest and short-lived condolences that

Maida Allen's private tragedy struck, and that her friends participated in their own version of pettiness.

From the outset, the author's inferences regarding the shallowness of Maida's constellation of erstwhile female friends is held before the reader's scrutiny. Despite the fact that Maida exhausted their energy with constant repetition of her sorrow, their abandonment of her was extension of the empty values and self-centeredness already catalogued as part of the times. The fact that "the most ruthless bore may still be genuinely in anguish" (p. 39) was not sufficient cause to summon Maida's friends back from the dereliction of their social duties.

When the day actually came that one lady slammed down her tea cup and shrieked "For Christ's sake, Maida, talk about something else" (p. 39), and the invitation to arrange social gatherings of male guests and mocha mousse ceased, and her friends finally gave up the whole thing, Maida concluded resentfully that luckily she had found them out in time—"in time for what, she did not state" (p. 39). But perhaps an answer for that will be forthcoming.

The reader must be careful not to be drawn in entirely by the sardonic humor of the situation. Indeed Maida is a flat, uninteresting woman, whose lack of acuity may have contributed to her own disaster, just as her obsessive self-pity contributes to her current dullness. But are the women by whom she is immediately surrounded any better? The desperate smallness of their values, the narrowness of lives revolving around ritualistic teas and "pleasant little dinner parties" (p. 39), where no depth of thought or conversation is encouraged or takes place and the hostess is forced to miserably accept "the host's ultimatum on who was not to be asked again" (p. 38), the constant diet of gossip and small talk that monotonously dissects the "saga of the deserted" (p. 38), and the need for males and male approval as their *raison d'etre*, expose the condition of women who are entwined with each other by the shared boredom of their lives.

They deceive themselves by deceiving each other, and their lack of loyalty, compassion, and depth are the consequences of their loss of self-respect. Like the woman of the opening passages, these women do not actively contribute or respond to the climate of intellectual stimulation or social growth as individuals.

As for Maida, the story is essentially a study of various levels of estrangement. Maida Allen does not know her husband and she does not know herself. Interestingly, there is little physical description of Maida. We gather that she is pretty and has, in her words, "proven talents as a wife, chum, and lover" (p. 39). As her present solitary state became more intolerable to her, she steered her memory back along the "sunny bypaths" of her marriage, to recall "eleven years of. . .perfect happiness" (p. 40). This delusion is quickly noted by the sober voice of the omniscient author, who points out that if she had eleven years of "perfect happiness, she was probably the only human being who ever did" (p. 40). In this view Maida perpetuates the same myth after Guy has left that she perpetuated while he was with her.

However, the author advises us with subtle hints that there were trouble signs in the marriage that Maida refused or perhaps was unable to recognize. Maida rationalizes that "Guy had a man's little moods, sometimes, but she could always smile him out of them" and, furthermore, that these minute differences only brought them closer together. With prosaic dullness she takes false comfort in the platitudinous notion that "lovers' quarrels was the way to bed" (p. 40). The reader learns later that Guy's version of their relationship, conversely, is rooted in deep discontentment and prolonged dissatisfaction with a marriage that had ceased to give him any happiness for the past six years. "I'd been saying it to you for six of those eleven years," Guy tells Maida in the last scene, but "you interpreted it as a cry of 'Wolf'" (p. 43).

Maida's ability to rationalize her husband's years of discontent, to dismiss reality from her life by avoiding the hard facts, to delude herself with Pollyanna eyes and saccharine words of "perfect happiness" (p. 40), are symptoms of an unstimulated personality blunted by tedium, unaccustomed to probing reasoning, and untrained in thoughtful introspection. Her marriage was a double trap: It not only dulled her personality through the cycle of tedious routine, but it dulled her capacity to see the pernicious effect of that on her husband and their relationship. In effect, Maida's atrophying existence has robbed her of the ability to analyze her own symptoms, and she happily presides over her own disease.[142]

Product of a flimsy world of fair-weather friendships, pointless communications, and superficial values, Maida was equipped to bring only the by-products of this conditioning to her marriage, as well as to her life in general. Now, bereft of friends and husband, Maida struggles in her loneliness to define what has happened to her. Parker furnishes insight into Maida's limited psychological and emotional depth in the following deceptive lines:

> She wanted to find understanding—that thing so many spend their lives in seeking, though surely it should be easy to come upon, for what is it but mutual praise and pity. (p. 40)

On close examination, it is not the innocence of the lines that impresses us, it is the ignorance. Certainly, it is true that "understanding" looms high as a priority in human relationships. But to conclude that this "understanding" could be achieved merely by "mutual praise and pity" and is "easy to come upon" is simply delusion. Yet the point is major. Maida's *gestalt* at this time does not permit her to probe the complexity of what was taking place. Nor is she capable of any emotion but confusion and self-pity.

However, she does begin to show some signs of growing spirit and imagination. With difficulty she assembles a fresh circle of friends who do not give her "understanding" but "exhortation" (p. 49). In the intimate afternoon sessions at her apartment, they advise her "to buck up, pull herself together, to get on her toes" (p. 40), a litany of imitative male colloquialisms from the emerging, new tough-minded women. When one woman advises Mrs. Allen to tell Guy Allen to go to hell, she discontinues the sessions, but not before meeting Dr. Marjorie Langham.

The previous scene, condensed into three short paragraphs, anticipated nearly a decade earlier some of the flavor and character of the women's movement that was to come. The "intimate sessions at her apartment" (p. 40), the aggressive voices of the women advising Maida to stand up to Guy in language that recalled "fight talk in the locker room" (p 40), and the bright female psychiatrist, Dr. Langham, are prophesies of the consciousness-raising session of the seventies, the bold new feminist language of identity, and the liberated professional women of the women's revolution. Drawn in broad satiric strokes, the resemblance to a social issue with which Parker had herself identified is there.

In 1957, the year the story was written, Parker told Marion Capron, "I'm a feminist, and God knows I'm loyal to my sex, and you must remember that from my very early days, when this city was scarcely safe from buffaloes, I was in the struggle for equal rights for women."[143] Little critical attention was given to Parker for these views at the time, yet it is clear that this story, in particular, reflected her own emerging feminist consciousness.

No doubt with this in mind, she cast the significant character of the psychiatrist as a female. Dr. Marjorie Langham, slender, smiling, self-assured, an enormously successful "healer of troubled minds" (p. 40), was perfect for Mrs. Allen. A woman of quick comprehension and generous sympathy for members of her sex, she practiced her talent in her own office filled with chintz and prided herself on a woman-to-woman relationship with her clients. It took her no time to diagnose Guy Allen's outrageous behavior in deserting his wife: "Those middle forties! That dear old dangerous age! Why that's the matter with him" (p. 40). This diagnosis was arrived at immediately, though Mr. Allen was never consulted as to its accuracy.

Parker's satire of women's language is squarely depicted in Dr. Langham's opening remarks, as she refers to Guy's malady as "dear old dangerous age," a phrase filled with lady-like euphemisms. It is the first identifiable dialogue from a named character in the story. As we continue to follow Maida through her sessions with Dr. Langham, we learn that Dr. Langham's great talent is her ability to provide an immediate, stylish, friendly, and supportive solution to all of Maida's concerns. That she reduces all problems to simplistic issues, generalizes unfairly, gives specious advice, is somehow overlooked by Maida, who indeed seems happy for all the doctor's shortcomings.

Parker depicts Dr. Langham as stereotypically female in her limited vision regarding the Allen's marriage. Her impression that Guy was a muddled up, middle-aged madman, that he was suffering for what he had done, and that he would return penitent and contrite, were clearly attempts to tell Maida only what she wanted to hear: Dr. Langham "had the ability to make wet straws seem like sturdy legs to the nearly submerged" (p. 41).

Dr. Langham effects her cure with Maida by giving her "the praise and pity" (p. 40) Maida wants, but paying perhaps too little attention to the diagnosis and treatment she needs. However, ultimately, Maida credits Dr. Langham entirely for her cure. The most interesting aspect to Dr. Langham's personality is hidden in the depths of her own psychological tissue, as the emergence of her anger toward men surfaces once Guy calls, an event we shall discuss subsequently.

The sessions with Dr. Langham provide Maida with what she believes is a viable medical explanation for her husband's desertion: male menopause. Dr. Langham explains: "He's going through the change . . . It's just the traditional case of temporarily souped-up nerves and the routine change in metabolism" (pp. 40-41). More importantly, Dr. Langham's assurance that Guy was suffering now and filled with shame and remorse, fortifies Maida's conviction that she was indeed a true, wise, kind woman whose patient vigil for her middle-aged, rebellious husband would be rewarded after he sickened for home and returned sheepish and mortified. The copies of the books given to her by Dr. Langham, written by women authorities on such matters, confirm this view. Furthermore, Dr. Langham insists that "he knows what he did to you—he doesn't know why he did it, the way we do, but he knows. He's doing a lot of thinking about you. His not daring to call you up shows that" (p. 41).

Maida has found a safe haven in Dr. Langham's counsel. Her willing acceptance of this female concoction continues to prevent Maida from true introspection. Maida would wait, not like the rejected flower of her early black days of misery, but like a brave and wise woman, with patience "for her poor muddled man to get through his little indisposition" (p. 41) and return home to her to be guided to recovery and restoration. What Maida's responsibility in this matter is remains conspicuously unaddressed by either of the women. Does Maida actually believe that all husbands in their forties who walk out on their wives are suffering from metabolic changes, as Dr. Langham convenietly suggests? Does Dr. Langham's advice that Maida wait until the penitent husband calls enable Maida to grow as an individual, or confront her life on a deeper level?

The sessions with the pansophical Dr. Langham fail to provide Maida with the slightest understanding of herself. In fact, she is completely exonerated and as blameless as she was in her early days of self-pity. Maida has merely pendulated between the polarities of dark depression and optimistic vigilance regarding Guy's desertion without any degree of self-analysis. By projecting the blame on Guy exclusively, both women implicitly collaborate in an indictment of men that is subtle but trenchant. In this way, the story begins to take on strokes of their combined muted anger against men, which becomes actualized in Maida's final carnivorous vision, the banquet of crow.

The shift from passive to active anger is occasioned by Guy's phone call to make arrangements to fetch his suitcase, regarded erroneously by Maida as his capitulation. The event, confidently predicted by Dr. Langham, releases a flood of stored vindictiveness in an exquisitely cathartic moment for both women. In Dr. Langham's instructions lie the seeds of Maida's revenge and the truth of their mutual attitude toward men:

> Now listen to me. This is important. Maybe the most important part of your whole treatment . . . Remember that this man has put one of the most sensitive creatures I ever saw in my life through hell. Don't soften up. Don't fall all over him, as if he were doing you a favor coming back to you. Don't be too easy on him. (p. 41).

Dr. Langham's direction to make Guy suffer: "Don't be too easy on him," finds a willing executioner in Maida: "'Oh-h-h, I won't' Mrs. Allen said, 'Guy Allen will eat crow'" (p. 41). Remarkably, these are Maida's first direct words in the story. Throughout, we have learned about Maida entirely from the multiple voices of the omniscient narrator, from what other characters have said themselves, and from what other characters have said about Maida. Maida's direct entry into dialogue at this point, and with these words, a highly disciplined device, strategically dramatizes her active transformation.

An additional significant aspect of this interchange is Maida's striking response to Dr. Langham's insistence that under no circumstances should Maida ask Guy to stay all night! "'Not for anything on this earth,' Mrs. Allen said. 'If that's what he wants, he'll ask me. Yes, and on his knees'" (p. 41).

Dr. Langham's mind leaps immediately to the issue of sexual needs, to Maida's role as a stereotypical mate. As a psychiatrist, does she reflect the pedestrian belief that sex is really what all men are after? Are Maida and Dr. Langham both a product of social conditioning that accepts sex as a determinant of a woman's value? As for Maida's response, does the image of Guy, "on his knees" begging for her body, titillate her sense of revenge? Of power? Interestingly, both women reflect on, and seem to acknowledge in their attitudes, a conventional image of women primarily as sex objects. By participating in this myth, they perpetuate the very thing they abhor and contribute to their own oppression. Hence, from this standpoint, the author directs the reader to view these women as foolish but willing victims of a system that maintains their sexual utilitarianism as foremost.

The final scene, which brings Guy and Maida face to face for the first time, poses the possibility of reconciliation, though through the network of subtle clues already hinted at, Parker has effectively told us that such reconciliation is impossible. If we accept the view that Maida has understood very little about herself until now, in this scene the reader will discover how little she understands about her husband. Indeed the reader also knows very little about Guy except that he came in one night, "spoke a few words" (p. 39), and left his wife presumably forever. He lives at his club, sends his estranged wife a check on the first of each month, which comes from his courtly banker, and is, according to Dr. Langham who has never seen him, going through male menopause.

His arrival at the apartment to get his bag is his first entrance in the story. The scene, a synecdoche for their marriage, embodies the lack of communication and misreading of emotions that have characterized their relationship.

The cumulative picture we surmise of Maida at this point is one of extreme confidence in the belief that Guy will ultimately be brought to his knees. Indeed she promised Dr.

Langham precisely that when she left her that afternoon. Guy's cordiality, polite compliments, and generally gracious manner do not hide the clear facts that he is quite content and happy with his life; nor does it disguise his intent to be done with this interlude and leave without incident. Maida, on the other hand, is unable and unwilling to read these signals, just as she has been unable to read her husband in the past. In response to her polite inquiry about accommodations at the club, Guy declares "I have everything I want" (p. 42). The phrase is laden with innuendo.

The ritualistic conversation is brought to an end by Maida's deliberate reference to Allen's last words when he left her: "'I don't want to do this any more Maida. I'm through'" (p. 42), an abrupt and ugly farewell speech, she claims, after eleven years of marriage.

What ensues at this point deserves careful examination. Allen's revelations that he had been thinking about leaving for years, that indeed he had told her that, that she "heard" (p. 43) but refused to believe him, and that she knew he was unhappy confirms in our minds the estrangement that has dominated their relationship. But it also confirms Guy's failure at communication.

Guy has joined the parade of men in the opening sequence who "spoke a few words, and then went out their doors and did not come in by them again" (p. 39). Despite Maida's blunted perceptions of her marriage, we cannot help feeling that Parker herself believed Maida was entitled to more than a "few words" (p. 39) after eleven years of marriage. Frequent and abrupt desertions were well known to Parker. Guy's terse and dispassionate desertion of Maida constitutes a subtle form of mastery over her life. The juxtaposition of their names, Guy and Maida—i.e., Guy, which carries generic male connotations, and Maida, which carries generic female connotations—hints at the representation of man as the deserter and woman as the deserted. This symbolic alignment may imply authorial concern with regard to the perception of husband/wife roles.

The reader's thoughts are forced back to the early lines of the story and to Maida's perception of the marriage as "eleven years of perfect happiness" (p. 40). Was it possible that the same marriage could be seen from such dramatically opposite perspectives? Or has Maida, out of female conditioning and female dependency, simply refused to hear what was unpleasant and disturbing to hear, insisting on her myth of a happy marriage.[144] The crucial question is finally posed by Maida herself. The long overdue conversation at last takes place:

> "Why are you unhappy?" she said. "Because two people can't go on and on and on, doing the same things year after year, when only one of them likes doing them," he said, "and still be happy."
>
> "Do you think I can be happy, like this?" she said.
>
> "I do," he said. "I think you will. I wish there were some prettier way of going it, but I think that after a while—and not a long while, either—you will be better than you've ever been."
>
> "Oh you think so?" she said. "I see you can't believe I'm a sensitive person." (p. 43)
>
> "That's not for lack of your telling me—eleven years' worth," he said. "Look, this is no use. Goodbye, Maida. Take care of yourself."
>
> "I will," she said. "Promise." (p. 43)

There are in these lines (which resemble some of the poignancy in "The Lovely Leave") a touch of reality and truth that cannot be found in the early stories of Dorothy Parker. Devoid of the trademark cynicism, biting sarcasm, bitchy wisecracking and slick humor, the scene is invested with a particular sense of the struggle of two people who have known each other as strangers for a long time and who awkwardly try to capture one instant of communication, even though there is "no use" (p. 43).

Guy's reference to the notion that in their marriage "only one of them" was happy does not exonerate him fully for its failure or his inability to communicate his unhappiness to Maida. His perception that he informed Maida for years that something was wrong with their marriage, that he was bored by their relationship, and that only one of them was happy appears faulty. Perhaps he is as deluded as Maida.

Maida's question "Why were you unhappy?" was not only unasked before now, but it was also unanswered by Guy. There is furthermore the suggestion in Guy's remarks that somehow

Maida will be better off without him, "better," he says "than you've even been." In this statement is perhaps an admission that he is not the one, nor does he care to be the one, to stimulate her growth as a woman. It is perhaps no coincidence that Maida's only creative act in the story, the gruesome fantasy of the banquet of crow, comes after Guy leaves. The seriousness of the conversation is deflated, however, when Maida, after some cursory reflection, reminds Guy as he waits at the elevator, that his real problem is that he's "middle-aged," to which Guy replies quite perceptively "I wasn't middle-aged six years ago" (p. 43). So much for Dr. Langham's diagnosis.

The reader is now faced with deciphering the meaning of Maida's final behavior. She had, as Doctor Langham instructed, acted with "perfect coolness and sweetness" (p. 43), but it was she, not Guy, who was suffering. The punishing meal, "The banquet of crow" that she had planned for her husband, he leaves untouched for her to consume. But she is not such a willing victim. Resorting to a talent that had become her dominant trait, she rationalizes "It must have been that Guy was still not over his common illness" (p. 43). He would be back when he came to his senses, she determines, and creates a fantasy of his return: "shabby, broken down gnawing at a leg of cold crow, which she saw with all its feathers left on it, black and shining and disgusting" (p. 43).

Emily Toth, perceiving Parker's subversive intent, sees Maida's fantasy as a healthy product of anger: "creative, cleansing, good for the soul. . . . As the story ends she is relishing that delicious fantasy, word made flesh."[145] Certainly it is true that the revolting image of Guy Allen feeding himself on this loathsome symbol of his contrition is a clear and punishing indictment of men and an original metaphor of damnation. But that is not where the story ends. Toth fails to explain the final two lines: "No. Fantasy was no good. She [Maida] went to the telephone and called Dr. Langham" (p. 43).

These lines are open to a number of interpretations. On the one hand, "No. Fantasy was no good" appears to mean literally that the fantasy fails. Maida, who can never learn, calls the psychiatrist for help and pathetically begins the cycle again, still believing her husband cannot live without her. On the other hand, the lines "No. Fantasy was no good" may infer that the "fantasy" was not good enough, in the sense that it was not sufficient retribution, and in view of Dr. Langham's directions to Maida, "Don't be too easy on him" (p. 41), Maida may see in the psychiatrist an ally to assist her in plotting a more effective vengeance. Hence, "she went to the telephone and called Dr. Langham" (p. 43). Finally, the lines "No. Fantasy was no good" (p. 43) may actually signal the end of Maida's long romance with illusions, and her call to the psychiatrist heralds a healthy gesture toward a life with more reality.

In any case, it is the image of the punishing fantasy that dominates the final moments of the story and one suspects that Parker's cryptic ending was part of the author's strategy to suggest the complexity and emotional depth of Maida's experience as a woman.

In "Banquet of Crow," as in so many stories before, she wrote about an experience that was close to her. The marital estrangement Parker may have feared was never realized. To everyone's amazement, Dorothy and Alan remained together in their relationship, fiercely protective and simultaneously punishing of each other. Clearly Dorothy and Alan could not be happy together or apart. Dorothy continually accused him of infidelities, that according to him did not exist. They lived modestly, both of them drinking more than they should, and writing as little as they could. The fact that they made their home where a great many gay men lived, and that many of Alan's friends were now homosexuals, gave weight to Dorothy's long held suspicious about him. Whether or not he slept with men, he was attracted to them. Ultimately, Dorothy adjusted to the crowd of gay people that hung around the house and sometimes actually befriended them.

They worried and argued a good deal about money. Dorothy continued to write for *Esquire*, but was finding it difficult to produce and meet deadlines. She attempted to teach at Cal State, where she described her students as illiterate and humorless. She was a poor teacher and could not communicate with her students. They disliked her as much as she disliked them.

Her life at home with Alan was spent quietly (they never owned a television set), or squabbling about a litany of long felt complaints. The friction in the house grew, as Alan's drinking increased alarmingly. He became slovenly, moody, and more aggressive. It was not unusual for him to drink all day, while Dorothy taunted him continuously about being worthless and never being able to make his own living. Alan, in an effort to escape had devised a trick bookcase with a hidden release and would often barricade himself behind the bookcase door to be free of her words or be alone. In a life that was already jagged and dissolute, both Dorothy and Alan became accustomed to the routine consumption of alcohol, sedatives, and barbiturates.

On June 14, Alan returned to the house carrying a plastic bag of dry cleaning, and said he planned to lie down. When Dorothy discovered him hours later, the plastic cleaning bag was draped around his shoulders, and his bed was dotted with Seconal capsules.

The coroner's reports stated that Alan had died of "acute barbiturate poisoning due to an ingestion of an overdose,"[146] and listed him as a probable suicide. Dorothy never accepted his death as a suicide, insisting that it was an accidental mishap.

As in the case of her father, Dorothy never attended the funeral. But it was clear the suddenness of Alan's death stunned her. As friends dropped in she appeared to be in a state of suspended emotions. Pendulating between anger and agony over Alan's abrupt departure, her behavior was disconcerting. A woman, who had liked Alan and only pretended to like Dottie, asked if there was anything she could do for her. Dottie answered, "Get me a new husband." After a stunned silence, the woman retorted, "I think that is the most callous and disgusting remark I ever heard in my life." Dottie replied, looking straight at the woman, "So sorry. Then run down to the corner and get me a ham and cheese on rye and tell them to hold the mayo."[147] Dorothy later claimed to be in shock.

In the period following Alan's death, she was numbed by grief and misery. She never set foot in Alan's room again and at the end of March, broke and bedraggled, she left for the East Coast. Back in New York, writing became increasingly difficult; she was lonely, drinking heavily, and sometimes drunk for days. She resisted people who tried to help and her eccentricities, now strange and discomfiting, drove away all but a few loyal stalwarts. She once complained to Wyatt Cooper, "Everybody

I ever cared about is dead."[148] On those rare occasions when she referred to her late husband, she said, choosing to romanticize their tumultuous years together and ignore their twelve years apart, "We spent twenty-nine great years together."[149] To what extent her gallows humor was reflected in that remark, we shall never know.

Alan was fifty-nine when he died. The younger Campbell preceded Parker to his death in 1963, his last desertion. Dorothy carried on to 1967.

In her final story, as in the wide range of stories throughout her career, Parker wrote humorously about female behavior; but roaring beneath the words was a serious summons to examine more carefully the complex emotional sub-structure of the women Parker created.

Notes

1   Dorothy Parker, "Such a Pretty Little Picture," in *The Smart Anthology*, ed. Burton Rasco and Groft Conlkin (New York: Reyanal & Hitchcock, 1934). All further references to this work appear in the text.

2   James R. Gaines, *Wit's End: Days and Nights of the Algonquin Round Table* (New York: Harcourt Brace Jovanovich, 1977), p. 76.

3   Marion Meade, *Dorothy Parker, A Biography: What Fresh Hell Is This?* (New York: Villard Books, 1988), p. 83.

4   Gaines, p. 119.

5   Simone de Beauvoir refers to this rage against stains, mud and filth as a housewife's obsessive battle against sin and Satan. "The maniac housekeeper wages her furious war against dirt, blaming life itself for the rubbish all living growth entails . . . Severe, preoccupied, always on the watch, she loses *joie de vivre*, she becomes overprudent and avaricious. She shuts out the sunlight, for along with that come insects, germs, and dust . . . She becomes bitter and disagreeable and hostile." She also suggests that this compulsion for cleanliness may have a "sexual tinge," i.e., the result of masculine neglect often resulting in coldness and frigidity. *The Second Sex*, trans. and ed. H. M. Parshley (New York: Random House, 1974), p. 505.

6   Horney explains that "There are women who choose a feminine delicate and weak husband. They are motivated by their own masculine attitude, although they often are not aware of this fact. However, they also harbor a desire for a strong brutal male who will take them by force. Therefore, they will hold against the husband his inability to live up to both sets of expectations and will secretly despise him for his weakness." *Feminine Psychology*, p. 124.

7   In the chapter, "Taking Care," Patricia Meyer Spacks observes that the "wise, benevolent, controlling woman, the eternal Mother, who comprehends even if she cannot communicate the meaning of experience, in her mind reduces all masculine accomplishment to the level of child's games. She is never openly contemptuous, only patronizing." *Female Imagination* (New York: Alfred A. Knopf, 1975), p. 157.

Spacks believes that this is a strategy for survival in a world that denies women social fulfillment and teaches them to regard themselves as inferior.

8 See Robin Lakoff, *Language and Women's Place,* for a detailed discussion of the laws of the ways in which women's speech differs from men's speech. Her definition of "women's language" as language "restricted in use to women and language descriptive of women alone" is seminal to this discussion. *Language and Women's Place* (New York: Harper & Row, 1975), p. 7.

9 Dolores Barracano Schmidt has noted in her essay on the "Great American Bitch" that the stereotyped "man-eating female in American literature . . . is always wife and quite often mother; she does not work outside the home . . . she is educated, but not intellectual; well-informed, but not cultivated; her house is usually clean, orderly, well-run." However, unlike Mrs. Wheelock, the "great American bitch," is generally "not a housewife in the sense of one devoted to domesticity." "The Great American Bitch," *College English* 32 (May 1971): 901.

10 Schmidt, p. 904.

11 Meade, p. xix.

12 Horney suggests, however, that in some marriages, "the wife will not tolerate fulfillment of her expectations by her partner, because her own craving for power does not tolerate her being overshadowed by her husband." Horney, *Feminine Psychology,* p. 124. In this sense, Mrs. Wheelock perpetuates a situation that serves to fulfill her need for control.

13 Unfortunately, "Such a Pretty Little Picture" is excluded from Parker's collections and is not widely know.

14 Meade, p. 100.

15 Leslie Frewin, *The Late Mrs. Dorothy Parker* (New York: MacMillan Publishing Co., 1986) p. 54.

16 Arthur Kinney, *Dorothy Parker* (Boston: Twayne Publishers, 1978), p. 39

17 Frewin, p. 78.

18 Ibid., p. 79.

19 Meade, p. 102.

20 Dorothy Parker, *Enough Rope* (New York: Boni & Liveright, 1926), p. 51.

21 Meade, p. 104.   22   Meade, p. 105.

23 Malcolm Cowley, ed., *Writers at Work: The Paris Review Interviews* (New York: Viking Press, 1957) p. 82.

24   Dorothy Parker, "Mr. Durant," in *The Portable Dorothy Parker*, rev. and enl. ed. (New York: Viking Press, 1973). All further references to this work appear in the text.

25   Marilyn French, "Joyce and Language," *James Joyce Quarterly* 19 (Spring 1982): 241.

26   Parker had been replaced in a publicized affair by MacArthur with Beatrice Lillie. Gaines, p. 76. Ultimately, MacArthur and Carol Fink were divorced in 1926. In 1928 he married actress Helen Hayes. Meade, p. 421.

27   Ironically, Parker unburdened herself to her male drinking companions, who "classified abortion stories as woman talk" and repeatedly suggested that she should "go home and sleep it off." Meade, p. 105.

28   Parker told Marion Capron, "I haven't got a visual mind, I hear things." Marion Capron, "Dorothy Parker," in *Writers at Work: The "Paris Review" Interviews,* ed. Malcolm Cowley (New York: Viking Press, 1958; reprint ed. 1974), p. 80.

29   John Keats, *You Might as Well Live: The Life and Times of Dorothy Parker* (New York: Simon & Shuster, 1970), p. 90.

30   See Nina Auerbach's perceptive discussion of "The Fallen Woman," in *The Woman and the Demon: The Life of a Victorian Myth* (Harvard Univ. Press. 1982), pp.150-184.

31   Dale Spender, *Man-Made Language* (London: Routledge & Kegan Paul, 1980), p. 32.

32   James Britton, *Language and Learning* (Coral Gables, Fla." University of Miami Press, 1970), p. 23.

33   Capron, p. 80.

34   Lakoff alleges that there are relatively few situations where one can safely address and deal with another as an intimate and the other cannot. "The paradigm cases are master-servant and adult-child." *Women's Language,* p. 237.

35   Frewin, p. 322.

36   Frewin, p. 88.

37   Ibid, p. 88.

38   In the *Portable Dorothy Parker* rev. and enl. ed. (New York: Viking Press, 1973), p. 99.

39   Kinney, p. 40.

40   Capron, p. 76.

41   Dorothy Parker, "The Wonderful Old Gentleman," in *The Portable Dorothy Parker,* rev. and enl. ed. (New York: Viking Press, 1973. All further references to this work appear in the text.

42   Kinney, p. 25

43   Frewin, p. 9.

44   Keats, pp. 18-19.

45   See Meade, pp. 18-34.

46   Frewin, p. 18.

47   Griselda was the medieval heroine who patiently endured many trials imposed by her husband to test her devotion. See de Beauvoir's discussion of female martyrdom and the Griselda prototype (pp. 326-30).

48   Bunkers claims that by "satirizing the Griselda and the Bitch, Parker criticizes the American society which has produced these stereotypes and forced women into them" (pp. 28-29).

49   Meade, p. 14.

50   de Beauvoir argues that young girls are obsessed with their appearances since they are nurtured to believe that they must always be "pretty in order to obtain love and happiness; homeliness is cruelly associated with wickedness, and one is in doubt, when misfortunes shower the ugly, whether their crimes or their ill favored looks are being punished." (p. 328).

51   According to de Beauvoir, if a father's love is withheld from a daughter, "she may ever after feel herself guilty and condemned. . . It is directly as men, that grandfathers, older brothers, uncles, playmates' fathers, family friends, teachers, priests, doctors, fascinate the little girl . . . The emotional concern shown by adult women toward Man would of itself suffice to perch him on a pedestal . . . Everything helps to confirm this hierarchy in the eyes of the little girl. The historical and literary culture to which she belongs . . . are one long exaltation of man" (p. 324).

52   Bunkers claims that by satirizing the Griselda and Bitch, Parker "does not merely intend these figures to be ridiculed, but that her criticism goes beyond mocking specific satiric types," to portray roles that have been dictated by society. Bunkers argues that Parker's work is decidedly more feminist in its orientation because of her particular use of stereotypes, For example, "Hemingway's Bitches, such as Lady Brett Ashley and Mrs. Francis Macomber . . . are not portrayed as women whose roles have been dictated by society but as woman who have chosen their own roles" (pp. 29-33).

53   Carl Jung, *Man and His Symbols* (New York: Doubleday & Co., 1964), pp. 26-31.

54   See Spacks's discussion in *The Female Imagination* of Charlotte Gilman's short story, "The Yellow Wallpaper" (pp. 268-78). The story records the descent into psychosis of a young woman of comfortable circumstances with a devoted husband and child. Misunderstood, frustrated,

unable to commit herself openly to a creative alternative from her duties as a model housekeeper, she escapes into madness, identifying herself with the woman she imagines behind the bars of the yellow wallpaper, emblematic of her psychological imprisonment.

55 Jung, pp. 288-90.

56 Toth, p. 6.

57 Parker, p. 239.

58 Dorothy Parker, "A Telephone Call," in *The Portable Dorothy Parker*, rev. and enl. ed. (New York: Viking Press, 1973). All further references to this work appear in the text.

59 Meade, p. 190.

60 See Lakoff for an analysis of the effect of such linguistic treatment of women, and the distinctions between "girl," "lady," and "woman." Lakoff claims that women achieve status in society by virtue of their relationship with men, not vice versa. *Language and Women's Place*, pp. 19-42.

61 There has been a tendency in the field of research on sex differences in language, to emphasize findings of difference between the sexes more than findings of no differences. Findings are often generalized far beyond the particular population studied into overall characterizations of "women's language." However, a number of sources that document ways in which language defines, deprecates and ignores women are now acknowledged as creditable. See Casey Miller and Kate Swift, *Words and Women: New Language in New Times* (New York: Doubleday & Co., 1975); Thorne and Henley, eds., Stanley; and Key. Though attention has been drawn in this study to language facts that show that females are discriminated against, linguistic research shows that males also suffer discrimination in the verbal environment (see Key's chapter "Discrimination Against Males, Taboo, and the Double Standard," pp. 54-68).

62 See Dale Spender's discussion of the determining power of the "Namer" and the "Named" (p. 169).

63 It is useful to note that God is H*e*, and that the generic pronoun for the human being is *he*. Non-human elements may be referred to as *he* or *she* depending on the perceptions of its given characteristics. See Ethel Strain Champs, "Our Sexist Language," in *Woman in a Sexist Society*, ed. Vivian Gornick and Barbara K. Moran (New York: Basic Books, 1971).

64 See "The Queen's Looking Glass: Female Creativity, Male Images of Women, and the Metaphor of Literary Paternity," in *The Madwoman in the Attic*, pp. 3-16. Gilbert and Gubar explore the paralyzing impact on women artists caused by the theory of patriarchal powers that deny women a claim to creative action.

65 According to Dale Spender, this competition among women for men and husbands has "been more by design than accident" (p. 137).

66 See Spender's essay "Politics of Naming," pp. 163-82.

67 Barbara Warren, *The Feminine Image in Literature* (Rochelle Park, N. J.: Hayden Book Co., 1973), p. 1.

68 Leonore J. Weitzman, "Sex-Role Socialization," in *Women: A feminist Perspective*, 2ed. ed. Jo Freeman (Palo Alto, Calif.: Mayfield Publishing Co., 1979), p. 105.

69 See de Beauvoir's detailed explanation of Man as the Subject, the Absolute, the Essential, and woman as the Other, the inessential, the incidental (pp. xix-xxxiv).

70 Ibid., p. 432.

71 Karen Horney devotes a chapter to the problem of "feminine masochism" and the psychoanalytic belief that women are masochistic by nature. She points out that where there is a "frequency of unhappy love," desertion, humiliation in sexual matters, masochistic trends are evident. For women, "The anatomical-physiological factors that may prepare the soil for the growth of masochistic phenomena" include menstruation, defloration, childbirth, the biological differences in intercourse, the possibility of rape and the greater physical strength in man. To this, Horney argues, must be added the importance of cultural patterns of conditioning, which she claims cannot be ignored in any analysis of feminine masochism. *Feminine Psychology*, pp. 214-233.

72 Karen Horney believes that sexual distrust, born out of two elements, resentment and anxiety, have damaged the relationship between the sexes. Man's fear of woman is deeply rooted in sex, yet he fears the sexually attractive woman. Although he strongly desires her, he also strives to keep her in bondage. *Feminine Psychology*, p. 112.

73 Keats, pp. 156-157.

74 Frewin, p. 147.

75 Dorothy Parker, "Big Blonde," in *The Portable Dorothy Parker*, rev. and enl. ed. (New York: Viking Press, 1973). All further references to this work appear in the next.

76 It is interesting to note in this vein de Beauvoir's suggestion that the entire tradition of marriage enjoins upon women the art of "managing" a man. "One must discover and humor his weaknesses and must cleverly apply in due measure flattery and scorn, docility and resistance, vigilance and leniency. . . . A husband must be granted neither too much nor too little freedom. . . . This is indeed a melancholy science—to dissimulate, to use trickery, to hate and fear in silence, to play on the vanity and the weaknesses of a man, to learn to thwart him, to deceive him, to 'manage' him" (pp. 523-24).

77   On the subject of the popularity of drinking for both men and women in the twenties, Frederick Lewis Allen comments that the "bootlegger, the speakeasy, and a spirit of deliberate revolt" made "drinking 'the thing to do.' From these facts flowed further results: the increased popularity of distilled as against fermented liquors, the use of the hip-flask, the cocktail party, and the general transformation of drinking from a masculine prerogative to one shared by both sexes together." Allen, *Only Yesterday: An Informal History of the 1920's* (New York: Harper Bros., 1931; reprint ed., 1964), p. 82.

78   With regard to the "revolution in manners and morals" of the twenties, Frederick Lewis Allen claims that the confluence of diverse influences—"the post-war disillusion, the new status of women, the Freudian gospel, the automobile, prohibition, the sex and confession magazines, and the movies—had its part in bringing about the revolution. Each of them, as an influence, was played upon by all the others; none of them could alone have changed to any great degree the folkways of America; together their force was irresistible." *Only Yesterday*, p. 85.

79   Horney points out rather interestingly, that the belief that woman is masochistic by "nature" functions "not only to reconcile women to their subordinate role, by presenting it as an unalterable one, but also to plant the belief that it represents a fulfillment they crave, or an ideal for which it is commendable and desirable to strive." Furthermore, Horney argues that women's erotic life depends on their accommodation to the image of mild expressions of masochism as their "true nature" while such qualities are discouraged in men. "Qualities like emotional dependence on the other sex (clinging vine), absorption in 'love,' inhibition of expansive, autonomous development, . . . are regarded as desirable in women but are treated with opprobrium and ridicule when found in men." *Feminine Psychology*, p. 231.

80   See Paula Treichler's discussion for further examination of this linguistic technique in "Verbal Subversions," pp. 47-61.

81   Frewin, p. 106.

82   Phyllis Chesler, *Women and Madness* (New York: Avon Books, 1972), p. 48.

83   Erwin Stengel and Nancy Cook, *Attempted Suicide*, 2nd ed. (London, 1958; reprint ed., Westport, Conn.: Greenwood Press, 1982), p. 20.

84   According to Chesler, "one study found that sixty-nine percent of attempted suicides in America are female and conversely, that seventy percent of completed suicides are male" (p. 48).

85   See Chesler's discussion on "The Female Rose and Suicides Attempts," pp. 48-49.

86   According to Horney, in "The Problem of Feminine Masochism," one sees that "cultural factors exert a powerful influence on women; so

much so, in fact, that in our culture it is hard to see how any woman can escape becoming masochistic to some degree, from the effects of culture alone, without any appeal to contributory factors in the ana-tomical-physiological characteristics of woman, and their psychic ef-fects." *Feminine Psychology*, p. 231. Horney's acknowledgement of the importance of the conditioning effect of the "culture complex" or social organization in which the particular masochistic woman has developed, together with the inherent anatomical-physiological-psychic factors in women's characteristics, seems relevant to an understanding of Hazel's conception of herself, and her punishment role.

87   There are a number of interesting correspondences between Emma Bovary and Hazel Morse. Both are sensuous women who are victims of their own misconceptions of romantic love. Surrounded by the will of others, used and unfulfilled, they are women without luck, who fail in their relationships with men and are driven to despair and voluntary death.

The description of Emma's death-bed scene is a parallel worth noth-ing: "Emma's head was turned towards her right shoulder, the corner of her mouth, which was open, seemed like a black hole at the lower part of her face; her two thumbs were bent into the palms of her hand; a kind of white dust besprinkled her lashes, and her eyes were begin-ning to disappear in a viscous pallor, as if covered by spiderweb. The sheets sunk in from her breast to her knees, and then rose at the tops of her toes, and it seemed to Charles that infinite masses, and enor-mous load, were weighing upon her." Gustave Flaubert, *Emma Bovary*, trans. and ed. Paul deMan (New York: W. W. Norton & Co., 1965), p. 241. Kinney suggests that the crusted spittle from Hazel's mouth "doubtless descends from . . . the suicidal Emma Bovary, from whose mouth at death trickles black bile; but Emma leaves a respectable hus-band, a doctor, and their daughter, Hazel lives, and has no one" (p. 137).

88   Capron, p. 76.

89   Dorothy Parker, "Horsie," in *The Portable Dorothy Parker*, rev. and enl. ed. (New York: Viking Press, 1973). All further references to this work appear in the text.

90   This touch of urbanity is classic *New Yorker* magazine-style lexicon, and no doubt was lost upon a less cosmopolitan or regionally outlying audience who would have no idea of what a "charlotte russe" was.

91   In this vein, it is of interest to note that Nina Auerbach's study of the Victorian cultural imagination and the myths of womanhood devotes an entire chapter to the subject of "Old Maids and the Wish for Wings." Auerbach points out that the spinster in fiction has usually been a common comic or grotesque Gothic caricature. Even when treated sympathetically, the old maid is clearly diminished and lacks authen-ticity. "The Victorian old maid, as commonly perceived, leads no armies

to heaven or hell. Grotesque out of nature, her very name reducing itself to a snicker, she is unwanted even by the devil." Nina Auerbach, *Woman and the Demon: The Life of a Victorian Myth* (Cambridge, Mass.: Harvard University Press, 1982), p. 109.

92   According to feminist thought, "the cult of beauty in women, which we smile at as though it were one of the culture's harmless follies, is in fact, an insanity, for it is posited on a false view of reality. . . The obligation to be beautiful is an artificial burden imposed by men on women." Una Stannard, "The Marks of Beauty," *Women in a Sexist Society,* ed. Vivian Gornick and Barbara K. Moran (New York: Basic Books, 1971), p. 203).

93   The question of beauty has been of central concern for centuries. Germain Greer noted that Mary Wolstonecraft in her well-known work, "A Vindication of the Rights of Women" (1972), stated: "Taught from infancy that beauty is woman's scepter, the mind shapes itself to the body, and roaming round its gilt cage, only seeks to adorn its prison." *The Female Eunuch* (New York: McGraw-Hill & Co., 1970), p. 47.

94   In Greek mythology, Galatea was the beautiful female statue made by the sculptor Pygmalion. Aphrodite granted his prayers that the statue might come to life. For further discussion of the Old Maid and Galatean stereotypes see Bunkers, pp. 29-30.

95   Camilla has a counterpart in another poor little rich girl, turned mother, Daisy Buchanan, in F. Scott Fitzgerald's *The Great Gatsby.* Reflecting on the birth of her infant daughter, Daisy, who has just admitted to Nick that she's "pretty cynical about everything," recalls that when she was told it was a girl, "I turned my head away and wept. All night, I said, 'I'm glad it's a girl. And I hope she'll be a fool—that's the best thing a girl can be in this world, a beautiful little fool.'" F. Scott Fitzgerald, *The Great Gatsby* (New York: Charles Scribner's Sons, 1925), p. 17. The correspondence between Camilla's "useless" and Daisy's "little fool," are striking and carry innuendoes about their respective view of females. Parker greatly admired Fitzgerald.

96   Bunkers, p. 30.

97   Only in the last decade with the appearance of such works as Betty Friedan's *The Feminine Mystique* (New York: Dell Publishing Company, 1963) have women begun to offer realistic evaluations of the frustration, anger, boredom, and insecurity they come to feel as wives who have supposedly been given by husbands everything they could possibly desire.

98   Bunkers, p. 26.

99   On the subject of the artificial images that affect the way we come to think of ourselves, Erving Goffman's study of gender behavior—mainly the ways in which women are pictured in advertisements—points out the social and political purposes served by advertisements specifically

as a re-enforcement of the notion of "depicted femininity." Goffman says "If gender be defined as the culturally established correlates of sex . . . then gender display refers to conventionalized portrayals of these correlates." *Gender Advertisements* (New York: Harper & Row Publishers, 1976), p. 1. Hence, both men and women are victimized by images of social situations and gender behavior that they know are not real life, but in some ways become the reality of the life we are living out.

100 Meade, p. 230.

101 Meade, p. 236.

102 Keats, p. 176.

103 Meade, p. 230.

104 Ibid., p. 239.

105 Ibid., p. 227.

106 Dorothy Parker, "The Waltz," in *The Portable Dorothy Parker*, rev. and enl. ed. (New York; Viking Press, 1973). All further references to this work appear in the text.

107 Sheila Graham, *The Garden of Allah*, (New York: Crown, 1970), p. 141.

108 For a penetrating and informative discussion of Parker's use of "verbal subversion," see Treichler, "Verbal Subversions."

109 Lakoff's definition of women's language" as "language restricted in use to women and language descriptive of women alone," is relevant here. The overall effect of women's language, as has been noted earlier, according to Lakoff, is that it submerges a woman's identity, keeping her in her place by "denying her the means of expressing herself and encouraging her in expressions of triviality." *Language and Woman's Place*, pp. 7-8.

110 Ibid., pp. 8-19. For a comprehensive discussion that probes the relationship among language usage and patterns of role specialization between men and women, consult Thorne and Henley, "An Overview of Language, Gender, and Society," in *Language and Sex*, pp. 5-42.

111 Barbara Bellow Watson, "On Power and the Literary Text," *Signs* 1 (1975): 113.

112 Treichler, p. 50.

113 Treichler suggests that the phrase "trapped like a trap in a trap," with its repetition of the word "trap" four times in two short sentences, is a simile that "mirrors the meaningless repetition built into ritualized interaction. . .In a metaphor of infinite regress, the vision of traps within traps undoes the innocence of self-presentation. Women, so that they may be trapped, must themselves be traps." She goes on to

point out that the notion of a "trap trapped in a trap encapsulates the story's duplicities; it is the essence of subversion" (p. 56).

114   Hellman, p. 107.

115   The reference to "Jukes," is to the descedants of a family of New York sisters who were studied for hereditary criminality. Hence, the partner is characterized as a "genetic deviant." Ibid., p. 52.

116   The notion of death fascinated Parker. During her years at *Vanity Fair*, she subscribed to two undertaking magazines, *Casket* and *Sunnyside*. She often used the obituaries to name her characters, and her books have death-related titles: *Sunset Gun, Enough Rope, Laments for the Living, Death and Taxes, Not so Deep as a Well*, and *Here Lies*.

117   According to Treichler, in the original 1933 *New Yorker* version, "There was I" reads "There I was." The change to "There was I" strengthens the view that the phrase is highly "self-conscious." "The inversion on 'There was I' embeds the 'I' within the complex repetitive location. The nominative 'I' as subject is compromised by the structure, trapped within it, and this transformation sustains the portrait of a woman physically and verbally trapped" (p. 56).

118   Treichler suggests that her age is the "thirty five years she has spent chained to her own body" (p. 55).

119   Keats, p. 174.

120   Ibid., p. 178.

121   Capron, p. 81.

122   Dorothy Parker, "Glory in the Daytime," in *The Portable Dorothy Parker*, rev. and enl. ed. (New York: Viking Press, 1973). All further references to this work appear in the text.

123   See Conventry Patmore's *The Angel in the House* (London: George Bell & Son, 1885), a verse sequence that honors the courtship and marriage of Honoria, a girl whose unselfish grace and servitude to her mate reveal that she is not only a model Victorian lady but literally an angel on earth. For further discussion of the pernicious effect of the "angel in the house" image on creative women, see Gilbert and Gubar's discussion in *The Madwoman in the Attic*, pp. 20-44.

124   Patmore, p. 73.

125   Gilbert and Gubar, p. 24.

126   Capron, p. 81.

127   See Juliet Mitchell's discussion of alternatives to true womanhood and male emulation in the form of lesbianism (pp. 118-19). Simone de Beauvoir's discussion of lesbianism (pp. 450-73) provides further insights into the "virile" and "feminine" types of homosexual relations,

noting that lesbian woman often seek in women "a lover to replace the male who has betrayed her" (p. 466). According to Sidney Abbott and Barbara Love, in "Is Women's Liberation a Lesbian Plot?" in *Woman in Sexist Society,* ed. Vivian Gornick and Barbara K. Moran (New York: Basic Books, 1971), "The driving career woman, the feminist, and the lesbian are women who have struggled to reject male dominance" (p. 607). In this study, the authors suggest that lesbian women have an early history of independent and aggressive behavior and though they are not necessarily "male-haters," they have chosen to free themselves from male domination.

128   Dale Spender observes that "Woman live under the reality of the dominant group." While women "may appreciate the parameters of male reality, men frequently cannot appreciate the dimension of female reality." Women "see more" but must defer to the definition of the dominant group as knowing better. Applying the theory of a dominant/ muted group, women are expected to have a "disposition to find in favor of males and consider it logical to interpret the world in a sexiest way" (p. 90).

129   Ibid.

130   Dorothy Parker, "The Lovely Leave," in *The Portable Dorothy Parker,* rev. and enl. ed. (New York: Viking Press, 1973). All further references to this work appear in the text.

131   Meade, p. 328.

132   The presentation of women as divided beings continues to be a well known theme in women's writing as noted earlier. Kate Chopin in *The Awakening,* first published in 1899 (New York: Capricorn, 1964), writes of her heroine that "at a very early period she had apprehended instinctively the dual life—that outward existence which conforms, the inward life which questions" (p. 35).

133   According to Christine Pierce, "the essential content of woman's role is probably best characterized by the concept of 'support'. . .As long as women as a class play supportive roles, they contribute to the efficiency of a power structure that keeps freedom of role choice for itself." "Natural Law Language and Woman," in Woman *in a Sexist Society,* ed. Vivian Gornick and Barbara K. Moran (New York: Basic Books, 1971), p. 249.

134   It is of interest, "writes Lakoff, "to note that men's language is increasingly being used by women, but women's language is not being adopted by men apart from those who reject the American masculine image [for example homosexuals] . . . The language of the favored group, the group that holds the power, along with its nonlinguistic behavior, is generally adopted by the other group, not vice versa." *Language and Woman's Place,* p. 10.

135   See Vivian Gornick's essay, "Woman as Outsider," where she claims that in every sense a woman is an outsider distanced "from the center

of self-realizing life . . . Her inner life—no matter who she is—is, in many sense, ruled by the continual measure she is taking of her ability—on a scale of one to ninety million—to attract men. When she feels this power waning she literally feels that life is leaving her." In *Woman in a Sexist Society,* ed. Vivian Gornick and Barbara K. Moran (New York: Basic Books, 1971), pp. 126-40.

136   There is a fresh, serious voice in this passage, relatively free of Parker's usual broad satire of women's language. As a war wife herself in 1943, Parker could feel a measure of authenticity in this statement. Interestingly, Mimi returns to the female euphemism "But oh, it was lovely" in the last lines (p 18).

137   Readers Digest, September, 1944, pp. 79-80.

138   Keats, p. 243.

139   Meade, p. 328.

140   Dorothy Parker, "The Banquet of Crow," *New Yorker,* 14 December 1957, pp. 39-43. All further references to this work appear in the text.

141   Meade, p. 341.

142   Simone de Beauvoir points out that the tragedy of married life is that it dooms women to repetition and routine. Since real activities, earning a living and real work are the prerogatives of the man, the woman merely occupies herself with trivial things and gives herself entirely to her husband, though he does not assume the corresponding obligation (pp. 534-35).

143   Capron, p. 77.

144   According to Jessie Bernard's analysis of happy marriage, "some clinicians are now seriously questioning whether the qualities that are associated with marital happiness for women may not themselves be contrary to good health." Among things noted in recent testing were that happily married women were docile, indecisive, cautious and not very self-sufficient. "They were, in brief, women who had achieved an 'adjustment' standard of mental health. They fit the situation they had been trained from infancy to fit and enjoyed conformity to it." "The Paradox of the Happy Marriage," in *Women in a Sexist Society,* ed. Vivian Gornick and Barbara K. Moran (New York: Basic Books, 1971), p. 157.

145   Toth, p. 76.

146   Meade, p. 393.

147   Frewin, p. 289.

148   Meade, p. 406.

149   Frewin, p. 293.

Afterword

The interpretations in this work exist to celebrate the significance of Dorothy Parker's contribution to feminist thinking. The critical canon at large seems to have ignored the serious role that women portrayed in the evolution of Parker's art. The stories discussed here attempt to explore the inner world of women's lives as a place of buried conflicts; a fictive universe where women attempt to define themselves and their relationships with men, a place of comic failure, where there is little laughter that does not hurt.

All of the stories deal with issues which at their core are concerned ultimately with the way women respond to the dominion of a patriarchal environment. The value in examining the lives of these fictional people serve to heighten our perceptions in surprising and unpredictable ways, when we approach the ostensible superficialities of their existence with patient and persisting probing.

Duplicity, aggression, anger, cruelty, exploitation, depression, abuse, affection, hypocrisy and a reservoir of emotional currents abound in the female realms beneath the surface of the satiric language. A close fresh reading of Parker's characterization of women reveals sometimes so unexpectedly, the social and psychological forces at work both implicitly and explicitly, that contribute to these levels of female behavior.

In addition to her technical virtuosity as a writer, there is the compelling image of Parker herself, an artist who drew from the disharmony and blemishes of her life to model the characters of her fiction. Throughout her life, as we have seen, Parker examined women through cynical sardonic eyes. Yet as contemporary critics, we are wise to regard her work as insightful testimonies about the realities, not the absurdities, of the female experience.

Young, single, married, middle-aged, elderly women came under the scrutiny as did their relationships with husbands, partners, lovers, fathers, family and other females. Her humor does not conceal from the penetrating eye, the details of painfulness that she observed in these relationship or the absence of happiness.

Much has been said in this study about the impact of a patriarchal society on the lives of women, and the lack of options open to women in these works. However, Parker also, it seems, acknowledges that women contribute to the cause of their own anguish, whether they choose to knowingly or unknowingly.

The writer, especially a woman writer, who takes a female as a subject, distinguishes women by the artistic attention she gives to them. By not averting her eyes to the importance of female experience, even, or perhaps, especially, when that experience is small or trivial, she encourages the nuances of our understanding as readers. Parker teaches us about women not by sympathizing with their plight, but by portraying the female experience, even in its most frivolous moments, and allowing us exquisite entry to feminine awareness.

It is possible today to read with interest about women as legitimate and accepted subjects. Even in the ironic stereotypes that Parker envisioned, she held out the opportunity for modern feminist thinkers to examine the boundaries that constrict women. It is difficult to alter formative views of fiction against old assumptions and interpretations. The fiction of Parker, attached as it was to the life of Parker, are part of a larger cultural system that dominated the writer, her work, and the period in which she lived. Th limitations imposed by previous traditional views regarding the women in her work, deserve to stand corrected.

Toward this end, this study re-visits the experiences of a small group of very particular American literary women and re-evaluates the narrow but meaningful world in which they lived.

Bibliography

Primary Sources

Parker, Dorothy. *After Such Pleasures*. New York: Viking, 1933.

———. "The Banquet of Crow." *New Yorker*, 14 December 1975, pp. 39–43.

———. *The Best of Dorothy Parker*. London: Methuen, 1952.

———. *Close Harmony*, with Elmer L. Rice. New York: Samuel French, 1929.

———. *Collected Poetry of Dorothy Parker*. New York: Modern Library, 1942.

———. *Collected Stories of Dorothy Parker*. New York: Modern Library, 1942.

———. *Constant Reader*. New York: Viking, 1970.

———. *Death and Taxes*. New York: Viking, 1931.

———. *Enough Rope*. New York: Boni & Liveright, 1926.

———. *Here Lies*. New York: Viking, 1939.

———. *The Ladies of the Corridor*, with Arnaud d'Usseau. New York: Viking, 1954.

———. *Laments for the Living*. New York: Viking, 1930.

———. *Not So Deep as a Well*. New York: Viking, 1936.

———. *The Portable Dorothy Parker*. Rev. and enl. ed. New York: Viking Press, 1973.

———. *Short Story: A Thematic Anthology*, with Frederick B. Shroyer. New York: Charles Scribner's Sons, 1965.

——. "Such a Pretty Little Picture." In *The Smart Set Anthology*, pp. 158–166. Edited by Burton Rasco and Groff Conklin. New York: Reynal & Hitchcock, 1934

——. *Sunset Gun*. New York: Boni & Liveright, 1928.

——. *The Viking Portable Dorothy Parker*. New York: Viking, 1944.

——. "Who Is That Man?" *Readers' Digest*, September 1947, pp. 79–80.

Recordings by Parker

——. *Dorothy Parker: Poems and "Horsie."* Spoken Arts 726.

——. *The World of Dorothy Parker*. Verse V-15029.

Secondary Sources

Historical and Biographical Background

Adams, Franklin P. "Dorothy Parker." In *Writers at Work: The Paris Review Interviews*, p. 72. Edited by Malcolm Cowley. New York: Viking, 1969.

Adams, Samuel Hopkins. *A Woolcott: His Life and His World*. New York: Reynal & Hitchcock, 1945.

Allen, Frederick Lewis. *The Big Change: America Transforms Itself 19001950*. New York: Harper & Row, 1958.

——. *Only Yesterday: An Informal History of the 1920's*. New York: Harper Bros., 1931; reprint ed., 1964.

——. *Since Yesterday*. New York: Bantam Books, Harper Bros., 1939; reprint ed., 1972.

Beach, J. W. *American Fiction*. New York: Macmillan, 1941.

Benchley, Nathaniel. *Robert Benchley*. New York: McGraw-Hill, 1953.

Bentley, E. R. *The Dramatic Event*. Boston: Beacon Press, 1954.

Capron, Marion. "Dorothy Parker," In *Writer at Work: The "Paris Review" Interviews*, pp. 69–82. Edited by Malcolm Cowley. New York: Viking Press, 1958; reprint ed., 1979.

Cooper, Morton. "Men seldom make passes / At girls who wear glasses." *Diners' Club Magazine*, October 1964, p. 46.

Cooper, Wyatt. "Whatever you think Dorothy Parker was like, she wasn't." *Esquire*, July 1968, p. 56.

Cowley, Malcolm, ed. *Writers at Work: The Paris Review Interviews*. New York: Viking Press, 1957.

Crowninshield, Frank. "Crowninshield in the Cub's Den." *Vogue*, 15 September 1944, pp. 162–63, 107–201.

"Dorothy Parker Recalled as Wit." *New York Times*, 10 June 1967, p. 33.

Drennen, Robert E., ed. *The Algonquin Wits*. New York: Citadel Press, 1968.

Ephron, Nora. *Crazy Salad: Something About Women*. New York: Knopf, 1975.

Frewin, Leslie. *The Late Mrs. Dorothy Parker*. New York: Macmillan Publishing Co., 1986.

Gaines, James R. *Wit's End: Days and Nights of the Algonquin Round Table*. New York: Harcourt Brace Jovanovich, 1977.

Gill, Brendan. Introduction to *The Portable Dorothy Parker*. Rev. and enl. ed. New York: Viking, 1973.

Graham, Sheilah. *The Garden of Allah*. New York: Crown, 1970.

Gray, James. *On Second Thought*. Minneapolis: University of Minnesota Press, 1946.

Guiles, Fred Lawrence. *Hanging on in Paradise*. New York: McGraw- Hill, 1975.

Harriman, Margaret Case. *The Vicious Circle*. New York: Rinehart, 1951.

Hellman, Lillian. *An Unfinished Woman: A Memoir*. Boston: Little, Brown, & Co., 1969.

Keats, John. *You Might as Well Live: The Life and Times of Dorothy Parker*. New York: Simon & Schuster, 1970.

Kinney, Arthur. *Dorothy Parker*. Boston: Twayne Publishers, 1978.

Lauterbach, Richard. "The Legend of Dorothy Parker." *Esquire*, October 1944, pp. 93, 139, 141, 143, 145, 146.

Lawrence, Margaret. *The School of Femininity*. New York: Frederick A. Stokes Company, 1936.

Loos, Anita. *But Gentlemen Marry Brunettes*. New York: Boni & Liveright, 1928.

——. *A Girl like I*. New York: Viking, 1966.

Maugham, W. Somerset. "Variations on a Theme." Introduction to *The Viking Portable Dorothy Parker*. New York: Viking, 1944.

Meade, Marion. *Dorothy Parker, A Biography: What Fresh Hell Is This?* New York: Villard Books, 1988.

Obituary of Edwin Parker, *Hartford Courant*, 8 January 1933, p. 6.

Rascoe, Burton, and Conklin, Groff, eds. *The Smart Set Anthology*. New York: Reynal & Hitchcock, 1934.

Seldes, G. *The Seven Lively Arts*. New York: Sagamore Press, 1957.

Shannon, D. A. *Between the Wars: America, 1919–1941*. Boston: Mifflin, 1965.

Sheean, Vincent. *Personal History*. New York: Modern Library, 1940.

Smith, H. A. *Desert Island DeCameron*. Philadelphia: Blakiston Co., 1947.

Stearns, H. *America Now*. New York: Charles Scribner's Sons, 1938.

Thorp, M. *America at the Movies*. New Haven: Yale University Press, 1939.

Thurber, James. *The Years with Ross*. New York: New York American Library, 1962.

White, E. B. *The Second Tree from the Corner*. New York: Harper & Row, 1965.

Whitman, Alden. "Dorothy Parker, 73, Literary Wit, Dies." *New York Times*, 8 June 1967, p. 1.

Wilson, Edmund. "A Toast and a Tear for Dorothy Parker." *The New Yorker*, 20 May 1944, pp. 75–76.

——. *The American Earthquake*. New York: Garden City, 1958.

——. *Classics & Commercials*. New York: Farrar, 1950.

——. *A Literary Chronicle*. New York: Garden City, 1952.

Wolfe, Thomas. *You Can't Go Home Again*. New York: Garden City, 1942.

Woollcott, Alexander. *The Portable Woollcott*. New York: Viking Press, 1946.

——. *While Rome Burns*. New York: Viking Press, 1934.

Yates, Norris. *The American Humorist: Conscience of the Twentieth Century*. Ames, Iowa: Iowa State University Press, 1964.

General References and Criticism

Abbott, Sidney, and Love, Barbara. "Is Women's Liberation a Lesbian Plot?" In *Women in a Sexist Society*, pp. 601–21. Edited by Vivian Gornick and Barbara K. Moran. New York: Basic Books, 1971.

Alstad, Dianne. "Course Proposal: Images of Women in Literature." In *Female Studies II*, pp. 7–9. Edited by Florence Howe. Pittsburgh: Know, 1970.

Auerbach, Nina. *Women and the Demon: The Life of a Victorian Myth*. Cambridge, Mass.: Harvard University Press, 1982.

Beckson, Karl, and Ganz, Arthur. *A Reader's Guide to Literary Terms*. New York: 1960.

Beer, Patricia. *Reader, I Married Him*. New York: Harper and Row, 1975.

Bernard, Jessie. "The Paradox of the Happy Marriage." In *Woman in a Sexist Society*, pp. 145–62. Edited by Vivian Gornick and Barbara K. Moran. New York: Basic Books, 1971.

Bernikow, Louise. *Among Women*. New York: Harper & Row, 1980.

Bloom, Harold. *The Anxiety of Influence: A Theory of Poetry.* New York: Oxford University Press, 1973.

Booth, Wayne C. *A Rhetoric of Irony.* Chicago: University of Chicago Press, 1974.

——. *The Rhetoric of Fiction.* Chicago: University of Chicago Press, 1961.

Britton, James. *Language and Learning.* Coral Gables, Fla.: University of Miami Press, 1970.

Brooks, Cleanth, and Penn Warren, Robert. *Understanding Fiction.* New York: Appleton-Century-Crofts, 1959.

Brownstein, Rachel. *Becoming a Heroine: Reading about Women in Novels.* New York: Viking Press, 1982.

Bruere, Martin Bensley, and Beard, Mary Ritter. *Laughing Their Way: Women's Humor in America.* New York: Macmillan, 1934.

Bunkers, Suzanne. "'I am Outraged Womanhood': Dorothy Parker as Feminist Social Critic." *Regionalism and the Female Imagination* 4 (Fall 1978): 25–34.

Carnegie Institute of Technology, Pittsburgh. Department of English. *Six Satirists.* Pittsburgh: Carnegie Institute of Technology, 1965.

Chesler, Phyllis. *Women and Madness.* New York: Avon Books, 1972.

Chopin, Kate. *The Awakening.* New York: Capricorn, 1964. (Originally published, 1899.)

Clemente, Alfred R. "Stable Irony: An Analytic Model for Short Fiction." Ph. D. dissertation, New York University, 1974.

Cornillon, Susan Koppleman, ed. *Images of Women in Fiction, Feminist Perspectives.* Bowling Green, Ohio: University Popular Press, 1972.

Current-Garcia, Eugene, and Patrick, Walton R. *What Is the Short Story?* Glenview, Ill.: Scott Foresman and Company, 1974.

de Beauvoir, Simone. *The Second Sex.* Translated and edited by H. M. Parshley. New York: Knopf, 1953; reprint ed., 1974.

Diamond, Arlyn, and Edward, Lee R., eds. *The Authority of Experience: Essays in Feminist Criticism*. Amherst, Mass.: University of Massachusetts Press, 1977.

Dinnerstein, Dorothy. *The Mermaid and the Minotaur: Sexual Arrangements and Human Malaise*. New York: Harper & Row, 1976.

Dostoyevsky, Fyodor. *Crime and Punishment*. Translated by Sidney Monas. New York: New American Library, 1968. (Originally published 1866.)

Douglas, Ann. *The Feminization of American Culture*. New York: Hearst Corporation, 1977.

——. "Parker, Dorothy Rothschild." *Notable American Women: The Modern Period, a Biographical Dictionary*. Cambridge, Mass. and London: Belknap Press of Harvard University, 1980.

Edel, Leon. *The Modern Psychological Novel*. New York: Grosset & Dunlop, 1955.

Elliot, R. C. *The Power of Satire*. Princeton, N. J.: Princeton University Press, 1960.

Ellman, Mary. *Thinking about Women*. New York: Harcourt, Brace, Jovanovich, 1968.

Feinberg, Leonard. *Introduction to Satire*. Ames, Iowa: Iowa State University Press, 1967.

Figes, Eva. *Patriarchal Attitudes*. London: Faber & Faber, 1970.

Firestone, Shumalith. *The Dialectic of Sex*. New York: Bantam Books, 1971.

Fitzgerald, F. Scott. *The Great Gatsby*. New York: Charles Scribner's Sons, 1925.

Flaubert, Gustave. *Madame Bovary*. Translated and edited by Paul DeMan. New York: W. W. Norton & Co., 1965.

Forster, E. M. *Aspects of the Novel*. New York: Harcourt, Brace, & Co., 1927.

Freeman, Jo., ed. *Women: A Feminist Perspective*. 2d ed. Palo Alto, Calif.: Mayfield Publishing Co., 1979.

Freibert, Lucy. Letter to author, 23 July 1982.

Freidman, Betty. *The Feminine Mystique.* New York: Dell Publishing Company, 1963.

Friedman, Norman. *Form and Meaning in Fiction.* Athens, Ga.: University of Georgia Press, 1975.

Friedman, Sharon. "Feminist Concerns in the Works of Four Twentieth Century American Women Dramatists: Susan Glaspell, Rachel Crothers, Lillian Hellman, and Lorraine Hansberry." Ph. D. dissertation, New York University, 1977.

French, Marilyn. "Joyce and Language." *James Joyce Quarterly* 19 (Spring 1982): 239–255.

Freud, Sigmund. *Civilization and Its Discontents.* 1st American ed. Translated and edited by James Strachey. New York: W. W. Norton & Co., 1962.

——. *The Interpretation of Dreams.* Translated and edited by James Strachey. London: Hogarth Press, 1953.

Frye, Northrop. *Anatomy of Criticism: Four Essays.* Princeton, N. J.: Princeton University Press, 1957.

Gilbert, Sandra M. "Life Studies, or, Speech After Long Silence: Feminist Critics Today." *College English* 40 (April 1979): 840–863.

——, and Gubar, Susan. *The Madwoman in the Attic: The Woman Writer and the Nineteenth-Century Literary Imagination.* New Haven: Yale University Press, 1979.

——, and——, eds. *Shakespeare's Sisters: Feminist Essays on Women Poets.* Bloomington, Ill., and London: Indiana University Press, 1979.

Goffman, Erving. *Gender Advertisements.* New York: Harper & Row Publishers, 1976.

Gornick, Vivian. "Woman as Outsider." In *Woman in Sexist Society*, pp. 126–44. Edited by Vivian Gornick and Barbara Moran. New York: Basic Books, 1971.

——, and Moran, Barbara K., eds. *Woman in Sexist Society.* New York: Basic Books, 1971.

Greer, Germaine. *The Female Eunuch*. New York: McGraw-Hill Book Co., 1970.

Gross, Laila, ed. *An Introduction to Literary Criticism*. New York: G. P. Putnam's Sons, 1971.

Henke, Suzette, and Unkeless, Elaine, eds. *Woman in Joyce*. Urbana, Ill.: University of Illinois Press, 1982.

Highet, Gilbert. *The Anatomy of Satire*. Princeton, N. J.: Princeton University Press, 1962.

Hills, Rust. *Writing in General and the Short Story in Particular*. Boston: Houghton Mifflin Co., 1977.

Hoffman, Nancy. "A Class of Our Own." In *Female Studies IV: Teaching about Women*, pp. 14–27. Edited by Elaine Showalter and Carol Ohmans. Pittsburgh: Know, 1971.

Horney, Karen. *Feminine Psychology*. New York: W. W. Norton & Co., 1967

———. *Our Inner Conflicts: A Constructive Theory of Neuroses*. Edited by Harold Kelmar. New York: W. W. Norton & Co., 1966.

James, Henry. *The Art of the Novel: Critical Prefaces*. New York: Scribner's Sons, 1934.

Jung, Carl. *Man and His Symbols*. New York: Doubleday and Co., 1964.

Kaplan, Sidney. "'Featureless Freedom' or Ironic Submission: Dorothy Richardson and May Sinclair." *College English* 32 (May 1971): 914–17.

Key, Mary Ritchie. *Male/Female Language*. Metuchen, N. J.: Scarecrow Press, 1975.

Kerhan, Alvin B. *Modern Satire*. New York: Harcourt, Brace, & World, 1962.

Kramer, Cheris; Thorne, Barrie, and Henley, Nancy. "Perspectives on Language and Communication." *Signs* 3 (Spring 1978): 638–51.

———, and Treichler, Paula A., eds. *Women and Language News*. Urbana, Ill.: University of Illinois, n.d.

Labrie, Ross. "Dorothy Parker Revisited." *Canadian Review of American Studies* 7 (1976): 48–56.

Lakoff, Robin. *Language and Woman's Place*. New York: Harper & Row, 1975.

——. "Women's Language." *Language and Style* 9 (1976/77): 222–45.

Lasch, Christopher. *The New Radicalism in America, 1889–1963*. New York: Random House, 1965.

Lode, David. *Language of Fiction: Essay in Criticism and Verbal Analysis*. New York: Columbia University Press, 1966.

Lubbock, Percy. *The Craft of Fiction*. London: Scribner's Sons, 1921.

Manley, Seon, and Belcher, Susan. *O, Those Extraordinary Women 1/2 or the Johs of Literary Lib*. Philadelphia: Chilton Book Co., 1972.

McConnell-Ginet, Sally. "Intonation in a Man's World." *Signs* 3 (Spring 1978).

Miller, Casey, and Swift, Kate. *Words and Women: New Language in New Times*. New York: Doubleday & Co., 1975.

Millet, Kate. *Sexual Politics*. New York: Ballantine Books, 1969.

Milic, Louis, ed. *Stylistics on Style*. New York: Charles Scribner's Sons, 1976.

Mitchell, Juliet. *Psychoanalysis and Feminism*. New York: Random House, 1974.

——. *Woman's Estate*. New York: Random House, 1971.

Moers, Ellen. *Literary Women*. Garden City, N. Y.: Doubleday & Co., 1976.

Patmore, Coventry. *The Angel in the House*. London: George Bell & Son, 1885.

Perrine, Lawrence, ed. *Literature, Structure, Sound and Sense*. 3d ed. New York: Harcourt, Brace, Jovanovich, 1978.

Pierce, Christine. "Natural Law Language and Woman." In *Woman in a Sexiest Society*, pp. 242–58. Edited by Vivian

Gornick and Barbara K. Moran. New York: Basic Books, 1971.

Pratt, Annis. "The New Feminist Criticism." *College English* 32 (May 1971): 872–78.

Rich, Adrienne. *On Lies, Secrets, and Silence: Selected Prose 1966–1978.* New York: W. W. Norton & Company, 1979.

Richards, I. A. *Principles of Literary Criticism.* New York and London: Harcourt, Brace, & World, 1961. (Originally published 1924.)

———. *Practical Criticism.* New York: Harcourt, Brace & World, 1929.

Rose, Phyllis Davidoff. "Review of *The Female Imagination*," by Patricia Meyer Spacks. *College English* 38 (September 1976): 98–101.

———. *Woman of Letters: A Life of Virginia Woolf.* New York: Oxford University Press, 1978.

Rosenblatt, Louise M. *The Reader, the Text, the Poem: The Transactional Theory of the Literary Work.* London and Amsterdam: Southern Illinois University Press, 1978.

Russ, Joanna. "What Can a Heroine Do? Or Why Women Can't Write." In *Images of Women in Fiction: Feminist Perspectives*, pp. 3–20. Rev. ed. Edited by Susan Koppleman Cornillon. Bowling Green, Ohio: Bowling Green University Press, 1973.

Sanford, Fillmore H. "Speech and Personality." *Psychological Bulletin* 39 (December 1942): 811–45.

Schmidt, Dolores Barracano. "The Great American Bitch." *College English* 32 (May 1971): 900–905.

Scott, Ann Firor, ed. *The American Woman: Who Was She?* Englewood Cliffs, N. J.: Prentice-Hall, 1971.

Seidel, Michael. *Satiric Inheritance, Rabelais to Sterne.* Princeton, N. J.: Princeton University Press, 1979.

Shanahan, William. "Robert Benchley and Dorothy Parker: Punch and Judy in Formal Dress." *Rendezvous* 3 (Spring 1968): 23–34.

Sheehy, Gail. *Passages: Predictable Crisis of Adult Life.* New York: E. P. Dutton & Co., 1974.

Showalter, Elaine. "Literary Criticism." *Signs* 1 (Winter 1975): 435–60.

———. *A Literature of Their Own.* Princeton, N.J.: Princeton University Press, 1977.

Showalter, Elaine, and Ohmans, Carol, eds. *Female Studies IV: Talking about Women.* Pittsburgh: Know, 1971.

Solomon, Barbara H., ed. *The Experience of the American Woman: 30 Stories.* New York: New American Library, a Mentor Book, 1978.

Spacks, Patricia Meyer. *The Female Imagination.* New York: Alfred A. Knopf, 1975.

———. "Reflecting Women." *The Yale Review* 63 (Autumn 1973): 26–42.

Spender, Dale. *Man Made Language.* London: Routledge & Kegan Paul, 1980.

Stanley, Julia P. *Sexism and Language.* Urbana, Ill.: National Council of Teachers of English, 1977.

Stannard, Una. "The Mask of Beauty." In *Woman in Sexist Society*, pp. 187–203. Edited by Vivian Gornick and Barbara K. Moran. New York: Basic Books, 1971.

Stengel, Erwin, and Cook, Nancy. *Attempted Suicide.* 2d ed. London: Chadma & Hall, 1958; reprint ed., Westport, Conn.: Greenwood Press, 1982.

Strainchamps, Ethel. "Our Sexist Language." In *Woman in Sexist Society*, pp. 347–61. Edited by Vivian Gornick and Barbara K. Moran. New York: Basic Books, 1971.

Thorne, Barrie, and Henley, Nancy, eds. *Language and Sex: Difference and Dominance.* Rowley, Mass.: Newbury House Publishers, 1975.

Toth, Emily. "Dorothy Parker, Erica Jong, and New Feminist Humor." *Regionalism and the Female Imagination* 3 (1977/78): 70–85.

Treichler, Paula. Letter to author, 9 January 1982.

———. "Verbal Subversions in Dorothy Parker, *Trapped like a Trap in a Trap.*" *Language and Style* 13 (1979): 46–61.

Warren, Barbara. *The Feminine Image in Literature.* Rochelle Park, N.J.: Hayden Book Co., 1973.

Watson, Barbara Bellow. "On Power and the Literary Text." *Signs* 1 (1975): 111–118.

Weitzman, Lenore J. "Sex Role in Socialization." In *Women: A Feminist Perspective*, pp. 153–216. 2d ed. Edited by Jo Freeman. Palo Alto, calif.: Mayfield Publishing Co., 1979.

Welleck, Rene, and Warren, Austin. *Theory of Literature.* 3d ed. New York: Harcourt, Brace, Jovanovich, 1962.

Welter, Barbara, ed. *The Woman Question in American History.* Hinsdale, Ill.: Dryden Press, 1973.

Wisse, Ruth R. *The Schlemiel as Modern Hero.* Chicago and London: University of Chicago Press, 1971.

Woolf, Virginia. *Moments of Being: Unpublished Auto-biographical Writings.* Edited by Jeanne Schulkind. New York and London: Harcourt, Brace, Jovanovich, 1976.

Worcester, David. "The Art of Satire." *Modern Satire*, pp. 179–86. Edited by Alvin B. Kerman. New York: Harcourt, Brace, & World, 1962.

Index

Note: "DP" refers to Dorothy Parker.
References to notes are indicated by "n."